Navdanya, meaning 'nine seeds', promotes biodiversity conservation, biodiversity, organic farming, the rights of farmers, and the process of seed saving. One of Navdanya's founders, and outspoken members, is Vandana Shiva, an environmental activist, physicist, and author. Navdanya has worked for two decades with producer communities and brings farmers' organic produce in new and creative ways to your table.

EARTHBOUND

Navdanya's Guide to Easy, Organic Cooking

westland

westland ltd

Venkat Towers, 165, P.H. Road, Maduravoyal, Chennai 600 095
No. 38/10 (New No.5), Raghava Nagar, New Timber Yard Layout, Bangalore 560 026
Survey No. A - 9, II Floor, Moula Ali Industrial Area, Moula Ali, Hyderabad 500 040
23/181, Anand Nagar, Nehru Road, Santacruz East, Mumbai 400 055
47, Brij Mohan Road, Daryaganj, New Delhi 110 002

First published in India by westland ltd 2010

Copyright © Navdanya 2010

10 9 8 7 6 5 4 3 2 1

ISBN: 978-93-80032-89-4

Cover and Inside design by Mukul Khattar

Printed at Aegean Offset Printers, Greater Noida

 # Contents

 Introduction

Cooking from scratch is fast becoming a lost art, so to say. In some western neo-cultures, as the kitchen space is reduced to a counter where the microwave oven sits, and in busy, two-income families, across the world metros, where 'convenience foods' are being adopted for perceived lack of time, cooking from scratch definitely seems to be passé.

Yet, simultaneously, in the wake of rising health concerns linked to the kind of food we consume, many people are realising the importance of reconnecting to this lost art. We, therefore, could be or in some instances are witnessing a Renaissance of this form of cooking. Where best to turn to in this endeavour than our traditional dishes. Today more than ever before, our traditional dishes need to be revalidated — and our title is a tribute to that knowledge.

As cooking from scratch started taking a backseat, so too the rich diversity of regional cuisines with their varied uses of spices and ingredients have threatened to sink into a homogenous red gravy or be standardised through a uniform use of spices. Travelling south or north, in the mountain regions or the plains, one often finds signs for a 'Punjabi Dhaba' which serves the ubiquitous paneer or tandoori dishes instead of the local cuisine. This is why we have included pan-Indian recipes, some of which come from personal sources, into our cookbook. It is meant to reflect diversity at all levels: that of regional cuisines but also that of nature's granary. We all know today that a diverse platter ensures a diversity of nutrients for our body.

In the book, wholesome, traditional and not-so-traditional recipes have been selected and organised in a user-friendly way to help you choose exciting and nourishing dishes from breakfast to dinner.

The recipes also use a very diverse range of grains from the better-known wheat and rice to forgotten millets and pseudo-cereals. In fact, forgotten foods such as jhangora (barnyard millet), raagi (finger millet), kuttu (buckwheat) and amaranth have a far richer nutritional profile than wheat or rice. Buckwheat, for example, contains the full range of all eight essential amino acids, while also being rich in calcium and vitamins E and B complex. As for amaranth, its nutritive value has ensured that the FAO encouraged its propagation all over the world.

The collection of recipes that have been compiled in the cookbook are all special and, in a way, a collector's item. Cooking them from scratch using fresh ingredients from a known source and better still of organic origin will ensure that loved ones have a fulsome meal that provides the maximum nutrition naturally. First time chefs will have no difficulty cooking like their grandmothers, since proportions have been meticulously calculated and the methods clearly and simply spelt out. Experts will enjoy trying out the vast array of dishes from across India. Happy cooking, and bon appétit.

Maya Goburdhun

Know Your Ingredients

 # Grains

Amaranth (ramdana maarchu/chaulai): Amaranth is one of the most nutritious grains in the world. It is hailed as the food of the future because of its high productivity and nutritive value. Amaranth is a pseudo-cereal — it does not belong to the true cereal family (Gramineae or Poaceae) but its seeds have high starch content. The name amaranth is derived from the Sanskrit word 'amara' meaning eternal, deathless. It is also called ramdana (God's grain) and rajakeera in south India. There are a variety of species of amaranth, with *Amaranthus hybridus* being the one found in India. Grain amaranth is a majestic and colourful crop, often attaining a height of up to eight feet. The mature ears range in colour from various shades of cream and rose, to deep rich pinks. Most of the commercially important varieties have tiny, creamy-white seeds.

Grain amaranths were domesticated centuries ago and are reported to have been cultivated in Mexico by the Aztec and Inca civilisations. This crop is believed to have been brought by Portuguese traders from Brazil to the Malabar in south India, from where it subsequently spread to the Himalayan region.

For farmers in many areas of the Himalayas, it is a valuable commercial crop. They barter the grain for salt, rice, wheat, clothes and so on, or sell it. This grain finds its way to the markets in the hills and foothills of the region and is mainly consumed by the plains people during religious fasts.

The nutritive value of grain amaranth with regard to proteins, amino acids, minerals, vitamins and food energy is superior to other conventional food grains. Amaranth grains have 14-16 per cent protein, which is easily digested and assimilated. It is rich in the essential amino acid, lysine, which is rarely found naturally. It is also an excellent source of phosphorous, calcium, iron, beta-carotene and folic acid. Hence, it is extremely useful for increasing haemoglobin and alleviating blindness caused by vitamin-A deficiency.

Amaranth is a multipurpose crop. The tender leaves and shoots of the plant are relished as a green vegetable. In the hills, the grains are popped and mixed with milk and sugar to make kheer; or halva, without milk. The roasted and partially popped grains are milled into flour and used to make roti or fried in oil to make puri and crisp pakoda.

Barnyard millet (jhangora/sanwa/kuthiravaali): Barnyard millet was domesticated in India. Intestinal contents of excavated Egyptian mummies included, among other plant remains, recognisable grains of *Echinochloa colona*. Another cultivated barnyard millet *E. frumentacea* was domesticated in Japan about 5,000 years ago. It remains an important cereal only in the tropics or subtropics of India. It is cultivated in Madhya Pradesh, Maharashtra and Tamil Nadu and is an important crop in Uttar Pradesh, where it occupies around 230,000 hectares. It is grown as a rain-fed crop during the kharif season. In the hills of Uttar Pradesh, it grows in soils with very low moisture-holding capacity. The crop matures in fifty-five to a hundred days, depending on the variety.

In the Garhwal Himalayas, the grain is cooked in a variety of ways. Husked barnyard millet is cooked like rice to make jhangora bhath. It is usually eaten with fresh yogurt or dal, or cooked in mattha to make chencheda, which is a common food item in all Garhwali households. The grain is cooked with milk and jaggery to make a delicious kheer during festivals and special occasions. Barnyard millet also serves as fodder for milch animals to increase milk yield.

Bengal gram/chickpea (kala chana/kabuli chana): Bengal gram or chickpea, *Cicer arietnum*, originated in south-eastern Anatolia (Turkey) and reached the Indian subcontinent before 2000 BC. India, Pakistan, Ethiopia, Turkey and Mexico have the largest areas under cultivation. Around the Mediterranean and in the Middle East, the chickpea has significant local production. In South East Asia, the gram is occasionally grown in areas that have a dry season. It is grown in Punjab, Madhya Pradesh, Rajasthan, Uttar Pradesh, Haryana, Bihar, Maharashtra, Jammu and Kashmir, Ladakh and Andhra Pradesh.

Bengal gram is mainly consumed as a dry pulse. Green pods are shelled for the gram and eaten as a snack or as a vegetable. The seed husks are used to feed livestock and poultry. This gram is used to treat several diseases. Their nitrogen fixing ability is one of their most seminal contributions.

Black-eyed beans/cowpeas (lobia/sonta/ruansh): Two centres of diversity appear to exist for this species of beans, which contains wild and cultivated forms: one in West Africa and another in India and South East Asia. The black-eyed bean or common cowpea, *Vigna unguicalatus*, is widely distributed throughout the tropics and subtropics.

It is cultivated mainly in India and Sri Lanka and to some extent in South East Asia. In India, it is grown in Rajasthan, Uttar Pradesh, Madhya Pradesh, Andhra Pradesh and Tamil Nadu.

The plant is cultivated for seeds — shelled green or dried. The pods and leaves are consumed as a green vegetable or used for pasture and green manure. In India, the bean is used mostly as a pulse, either whole or made into a dal. The leaves may be boiled, drained, sun-dried and stored for later use.

Black gram (urad): A primary gene centre of black gram, *Vigna mungo*, is found in India and a secondary centre in Central Asia. In South East Asia, black gram is cultivated in northern Malaysia, the Philippines, Thailand and Burma. It is also cultivated in Bhutan, Nepal, Bangladesh, Iran and Kenya, but it is a major crop in India only. Black gram is cooked as a pulse, direct or in various preparations. Small amounts are used as cattle feed. It has some use as a green manure and in medicine.

Brown mung beans/moth beans (matki/moth): The brown mung or moth bean, *Vigna aconitifolia*, is a native of the Indian subcontinent where it grows both wild and cultivated. It is also grown in China, Sri Lanka, Africa, the United States and Thailand. Green pods and ripe whole or split seeds are all cooked and eaten. In India and the United States, brown mung bean is also grown for green manure, forage and hay, and as cover crop. The seeds are used medicinally in diets for fever, while the roots are said to be a narcotic.

Buckwheat (kuttu/phapra/ogal): Buckwheat, *Fagopyrum esculentum*, is another pseudo-cereal that is cultivated for its high starch content. The angular shape of the buckwheat grain is distinctive. It ranges in colour from shades of grey or brown to blotched black. The kernel is white, soft and porous. It is rich in the complete range of vitamins B and E and provides a high level of calcium and iron. It is also a good source of potassium and phosphorous. The plants, which flower profusely, are a rich source of honey, and hence buckwheat is a good 'bee plant'. The tender leaves and shoots of buckwheat make a delicious green vegetable.

Egyptian lentils/red lentils (masoor): Egyptian or red lentil or masoor, *Lens culinaris*, is one of the oldest pulse crops of the ancient cultivations of Western Asia, Egypt and Southern Europe. It is widely cultivated in temperate and subtropical regions, and in the tropics at higher altitudes, especially in the Indian subcontinent. In India, this lentil is grown in Madhya Pradesh, Uttar Pradesh, Bihar, Ladakh and Jammu and Kashmir. The husked, split seeds are used in soups, while the young pods are cooked as a vegetable. Flour from the ground seeds, mixed with cereal flours, is considered a nourishing food.

In parts of India, the whole seed is often eaten salted and fried. The entire plant, green or dry, makes excellent fodder and green manure. The seeds are a source of commercial starch for the textile and printing industries. The lentils are supposed to remedy constipation and other intestinal afflictions. In India, the lentils are used as a poultice on slow-healing sores.

Finger millet (ragi/nachni/mandua): Finger millet, *Eleusine coracana*, is the most widely grown small millet in India. It is cultivated in the hills of Uttar Pradesh and the Deccan region. The ear on which the grains are borne consists of a whorl of finger-like spikes. The colour of the ears and the plants can vary from green to purple and deep violet. The colour of the tiny ragi/mandua grains vary from orange-red to reddish brown and dark-brown to almost black.

Finger millet was probably domesticated in the Ethiopian highlands and introduced in India more than 3,000 years ago. It is now the staple diet of most households in the Deccan, where nutritious and tasty dosai, upma, steamed balls (muddé) and porridge are made from finger millet flour. Popped finger millet flour with jaggery and milk (hurihittu) is prepared during festive occasions in Karnataka. Malting of finger millet is a traditional process followed in India, mainly to prepare infant foods and milk thickener formulations. This is popularly known as 'ragi malt'. Since finger millet is high in calcium, it is an ideal food for children. In the Central Himalayas, roti made with this flour, eaten with vegetables or dal, makes a wholesome meal. Finger millet flour is also mixed with amaranth or wheat flour so that it doesn't break while making roti.

Green mung beans: The green mung bean, *Vigna radiate*, originated in India or the Indo-Burmese region and has been cultivated for several millennia. It spread in early times to most other Asian countries, and more recently, to other continents. Despite its present wide distribution, green mung bean never became a major commercial crop outside Asia. In most South East Asian countries, mung beans rank among the three main grain legumes.

The dried beans are prepared by cooking or milling. They are eaten whole or split. The seeds or the flour are used in a variety of dishes like soups, porridges, snacks, breads, noodles and even ice creams. Mung bean starch is extensively used for starch noodles and mung bean protein helps to fortify cereal flours. Most popular as a fresh vegetable in oriental cooking are sprouted mung beans. Crop residues are a useful fodder, green manure and cover crop.

Horse gram (kulthi ka dal/gahath): Horse gram, *Dolichos uniflorus*, is extensively cultivated in the drier areas of Australia, Burma, Sri Lanka, the Himalayas, Africa and America, and especially in India. As a pulse, the seeds are eaten poached, boiled or fried, whole or ground. In Burma, boiled seeds are pounded with salt and fermented, which results in a product similar to soy sauce. All parts of the plant are used as fodder and as green manure. In traditional medicine, the seed is said to be an astringent, diuretic and tonic.

Maize/corn (makkai): Maize, also known as corn, is a herbaceous plant domesticated in Meso-America, which subsequently spread throughout the Americas. After Europe made contact with the Americas in the late fifteenth and early sixteenth centuries, it spread to the rest of the world. Maize is the most extensively grown crop in the Americas. While some varieties grow as tall as seven metres, most commercially grown plants have been bred for a standardised height of two and a half metres. Sweet corn is usually shorter.

Maize, *Zea mays*, is widely cultivated throughout the world and the United States produces almost half the world's harvest. Other major producers are China, Brazil, Mexico, Argentina, India and France.

Pearl millet (bajra): Commonly known as pearl millet, bajra is currently grown on almost 10 per cent of India's food-grain area. Pearl millet, *Pennisetum glaucum*, is the major food crop of Rajasthan. This millet can be grown in sandy soils and hence assumes importance in the arid region of Rajasthan. The plant is also cultivated abundantly in the arid tracts of Gujarat, Uttar Pradesh, Karnataka, Maharashtra and Andhra Pradesh.

Pearl millet has multiple uses besides being a staple food. Its fodder is an important feed for milch animals.

Pearl millet is mainly consumed after husking. It is cooked just like rice, or is ground into flour and made into a thin or thick porridge in the same way as finger millet (ragi). The flour can also be made into cakes or unleavened breads. Roti are made from the flour during the winter, as this millet has heating properties. The grain is used to feed poultry and livestock. The green plant provides a useful fodder and it is sometimes grown solely for that purpose. The dried straw, which is inferior to that of most cereals, may be fed to livestock, but it is coarse and hard. The straw and stalk are used for bedding, thatching, fencing and fuel.

Pigeon peas/yellow lentils (arhar, tuvar): Pigeon peas, *Cajanus cajan*, originated in India and spread to South East Asia in the early centuries. It reached Africa in 2000 BC or earlier, and found its way to the Americas with the European conquests and the slave trade, probably via both the Atlantic and the Pacific oceans. It is now grown all over the tropics but especially in the Indian subcontinent and East Africa. In India, it is cultivated in Madhya Pradesh, Uttar Pradesh, Bihar, southern Gujarat, Rajasthan, Haryana, Punjab and in some parts of the western Himalayas, Andhra Pradesh and Tamil Nadu.

Pigeon peas are mainly used as a pulse, but in some places the fresh seeds and even pods are made into a vegetable dish, spicy soup or other side dish. The ripe seeds are eaten roasted too.

The plants are useful as tall hedges on dry soil and on the bunds of paddy fields. They are often grown as a shade crop, cover crop or windbreaker, and even as a support for the vanilla vine. After establishment, the plant improves the soil by its extensive root system, nitrogen fixation by rhizobium and mulch provided by fallen leaves. Pigeon pea plants may serve as host for silkworms and the lac insect. The branches and stems are made into baskets and used as fuel. Traditional uses as medicine are many: for example, the young leaves are applied to sores, on herpes patches and to alleviate itching.

Rice (chaval): Rice has the distinction of being the most extensively cultivated crop of the world. The approximate area under rice cultivation is 100 million acres and over 90 per cent of this is grown in southern and eastern Asia, which are also the most highly populated regions of the world. About 185-200 million tons of rice is eaten every year and it forms the staple food of about half the human race.

Rice, *Oriza sativa*, has been cultivated in India since ancient times. From a wild aquatic grass, Indian farmers, over the centuries, selected and cultivated thousands of varieties of rice. No other cultivated crop has been developed to such an extent, to fit thousands of ecological niches across the country, from the temperate, high hills of the Himalayas to the tropical lowlands and deep water and salt water marshes off sea coasts. India probably has the largest variety of cultivated rice in the word — it is estimated to be around 200,000.

Rice bean (naurangi): Rice bean is native to South Asia. It is most widely cultivated in India, Burma, China, Malaysia, Mauritius and Japan, and to a limited extent in the tropical parts of all continents. It is commonly known as naurangi (nine colours) in India, as the beans have the hues of several colours. Rice beans are usually boiled and eaten with rice or instead of rice.

The young pods, leaves and sprouts are cooked as a vegetable. The whole plant is used as fodder, a cover crop, green manure and as hedges. In Perak, Malaysia, the leaves are used with rice flour in a poultice applied to the abdomen for stomach ache.

Sorghum (jowar): Otherwise know as sorghum-bicolor, jowar is the most important cereal after wheat, rice and maize. *Sorghum vulgare*, is grown both in the kharif and rabi seasons. The crop is capable of growing in a variety of weather conditions. It can survive in harsh, dry climatic conditions as well as temporary water logging. Sorghum supplies a major proportion of calories and protein to large sections of populations living in the semi-arid tropical regions of Africa and Asia.

The threshed grain is ground into wholemeal flour, but grinding should be done as and when required as the flour tends to become rancid on keeping. The flour may be made into a thin porridge, a thick paste or dough by boiling in water. The seed coat may be removed by soaking or damping the grain and pounding it lightly, with frequent winnowing to remove the bran. But the bran removal results in a loss of 10-20 per cent of protein content. It is a multipurpose plant, with the grain and the plant both used as fodder for cattle.

Soybeans (bhatt): The soybean, *Glycine max*, is a legume native to east Asia. It is an annual plant, classified as an oilseed rather than a pulse, which has been used in China for 5,000 years as a food and component of drugs. It is a good source of protein because it contains a significant amount of essential amino acids. Soybean is also rich in the omega-3 fatty acid, alpha-linolenic acid, and the isoflavones, genistein and daidzein.

Soybeans are the primary ingredient in many processed foods, including meat and dairy product substitutes, and are used to make soy sauce. They are an important source of vegetable oil and protein throughout the world. The oil also has several industrial applications. The United States, Brazil, Argentina, China and India are the main producers of soybeans.

Wheat (gehun): Wheat, *Triticum aestivum*, is one of the most important food crops in India. It has been in use since the early civilisations and is an integral part of rituals which have been documented in ancient Indian texts and scriptures. It is the staple in the northern regions of India, especially the Indo-Gangetic plains. Belonging to the family Gramineae, its traditional Indian name is kanak, exemplifying the golden colour of the seed. It is easily transported and stored and is used to produce a large variety of foods that include several types of breads, cakes, noodles, crackers, breakfast foods, biscuits, cookies and confectionary items.

It is a rich source of the entire vitamin B complex range, except B12.

The structure of the wheat grain is complex. Its main components are the bran, the endosperm and the germ. The bran is the outermost and toughest part of the grain. It protects the germ and endosperm from the weather, mould, bacteria, etc. It is a source of roughage, iron and protein. The endosperm, which is technically meant to provide food for the growing seed, is a rich source of carbohydrates. White flour is produced from the endosperm. The germ of the grain contains fat and vitamin E. So the complete grain, with all three parts, forms a comprehensive source of nutrition. Unfortunately, modern milling techniques remove the nutritious outer layer of the endosperm and the germ to produce white flour, which is mainly starch, empty of proteins.

 # Vegetables

Amaranth (cholai bhaaji): Amaranth is also known as pigweed. People around the world value amaranth as a leaf vegetable and a cereal.

In Karnataka, the leaves are used to prepare hulli, palya, maggigayhulli and so on. In Tamil Nadu, it is regularly consumed as a favourite dish, where the greens are steamed and mashed with a light seasoning of salt, red chillies and cumin. It is called keerai masial. In Andhra Pradesh, this leaf is added to the preparation of a popular dal called thotakura pappu. The Chinese use them as a stir-fry, and is called yin choi, while the Vietnamese convert it into a soup. In Greece, green amaranth is boiled and served with a dressing of olive oil and lemon, like a salad, usually with fried fish. The Greeks stop harvesting the usually wild-grown plant when it starts to bloom towards the end of August.

Amaranth greens, are a common leafy vegetable throughout the tropics and in many warm temperate regions. It is very popular in India. Amaranth is a good source of vitamins A, K, B6 and C, and minerals like calcium, iron, magnesium, phosphorus, potassium, zinc, copper and manganese. However, their moderately high content of oxalic acid inhibits the absorption of calcium and zinc, which also means that they should be avoided or eaten in moderation by people with kidney disorders, gout, or rheumatoid arthritis.

Reheating cooked amaranth greens is often discouraged, particularly for consumption by small children, as, similar to spinach, the nitrates in the leaves can get converted to nitrites.

Aubergine (baingan): Aubergine, brinjal or baingan, *Solanum melongena* is often referred to as eggplant owing to its shape. It belongs to the Solanaceae family, also commonly known as nightshades, is related to the tomato, bell pepper and potato, and grows several feet in height. While the different varieties differ slightly in taste and texture, one can generally describe the aubergine as having a pleasantly bitter taste and spongy texture.

The ancient ancestors of aubergine grew wild in India and were first cultivated in China in the fifth century BC. Aubergine was introduced to Africa before the Middle Ages and then into Italy, the country with which it has long been associated, in the fourteenth century. It subsequently spread throughout Europe and the Middle East. Today, Italy, Turkey, Egypt, China and Japan are the leading growers of aubergine.

Aubergine is a very good source of dietary fibre, potassium, manganese, copper and thiamine (vitamin B1). It is also a good source of vitamin B6, folate, magnesium and niacin. Aubergine contains phyto-nutrients such as phenolic compounds like caffeic and chlorogenic acid, and flavonoids like nasunin. Nasunin is a potent antioxidant and free radical scavenger that has been shown to protect cell membranes from damage. Several plants form such compounds to protect themselves against oxidative stress from exposure to the elements as well as from infection by bacteria and fungi.

Bottle gourd/vegetable marrow (ghia/lauki): Bottle gourd, *Lagenaria siceraria,* has multiple uses around the world. In the Caribbean its varieties are used as utensils, such as cups, bowls and basins, in rural areas. It can be used to carry water, or items such as fish, while out fishing. In some Caribbean countries, it is worked, painted and decorated as shoulder bags or other items by artisans, and sold to tourists. In parts of India, the dried, un-punctured gourd is used as a float (called surai-kuduvai in Tamil) to learn swimming in rural areas. The dried and cored thick outer skin has traditionally been used to make musical instruments like the tanpura, veena, etc. It belongs to the Cucurbitaceae family.

Bottle gourd has been grown since time immemorial and it is probably one of the earliest vegetables cultivated by man. It appears to have originated in Africa, where it grows spontaneously, as it does in India. It is now widely cultivated throughout the tropics, especially India, Sri Lanka, Indonesia, Malaysia, the Philippines, China, tropical Africa and South America. The bottle gourd is a warm season crop and grows best in a warm, humid climate.

The cooked vegetable is cooling, a diuretic, sedative and anti-bilious. It contains about 96 per cent water, which provides a feeling of relaxation after eating it. Bottle gourd is valuable in treating urinary and stomach disorders, since it is alkaline. A glass of fresh juice prepared by grating the fruit and mixing it with a teaspoon of lime juice reduces the burning sensation in the urinary tract due to high urine acidity. It is also useful in the treatment of stomach acidity, indigestion, ulcers and constipation. A pinch of salt added to the juice helps to curb extreme thirst caused by severe diarrhoea, diabetes or excessive intake of fatty or fried foods. In summer, it prevents loss of sodium, quenches the thirst and helps to mitigate fatigue. It is used in the treatment of insanity, epilepsy and other nervous diseases, and a mixture of the juice and sesame oil massaged into the scalp at night is effective against insomnia. Bottle gourd is not only rich in essential minerals, iron, protein and trace elements, it is also a good source of fibre. Several digestive problems like constipation, flatulence and even piles are caused due to lack of fibre in the modern diet. Hence diets using different preparations made with this vegetable are useful.

Cabbage (band gobi): Cabbage, *Brassica oleracea*, a member of the Cruciferae family, is related to kale, broccoli, collards and Brussels sprouts. Cabbage has a round shape and is composed of superimposed leaf layers. There are three major types of cabbage: green, red and Savoy. The colour of green cabbage ranges from pale to dark green, while red cabbage has leaves that are either crimson or purple with white veins running through them. Both green and red cabbage have smooth-textured leaves. The leaves of Savoy cabbage are more ruffled and yellow-green in colour. Because the inner leaves are protected from sunlight by the surrounding ones, they are often lighter in colour. Red and green cabbage have a more defined taste and crunchy texture compared to the Savoy cabbage's more delicate nature. All are great ingredients for salads.

Cabbage has a long history of use both as a food and as medicine. It is believed that wild cabbage was brought to Europe around 600 BC by groups of Celtic wanderers. It was grown in Ancient Greece and Rome where it was held in high regard as a general panacea, capable of treating a host of health conditions. The consumption of cabbage is reported to optimise the detoxification and cleansing of cells. The phyto-nutrients in the vegetable result in the production of enzymes involved in detoxification. Consumption of cruciferous vegetables, such as cabbage, is known to reduce the risk of several cancers, especially lung, colon, breast, ovarian and bladder cancer. New research reveals that crucifers provide significant cardiovascular benefits as well.

Cabbage is an excellent source of vitamin C. It is also a rich in fibre, vitamin A, folate, thiamin (vitamin B1), riboflavin (vitamin B2), vitamin B6, manganese, calcium, potassium, magnesium and omega-3 fatty acids. It contains phyto-chemicals called indoles and sulphoraphane, the breakdown products of compounds called glucosinolates.

Capsicum (Shimla mirch): Capsicums, *Capsicum frutescens*, also called bell peppers or sweet peppers, are like Christmas ornaments in the vegetable world. They are beautifully shaped, glossy and come in a variety of vivid colours — green, red, yellow, orange, purple, brown and black. Similar to their relatives, the chilli peppers, capsicums originated in South America with seeds of a wild variety dating back to 5000 BC. Like many other foods native to this region, sweet peppers were carried throughout the world by the Spanish and Portuguese explorers who travelled across this continent.

Since capsicums are very adaptable plants, growing in tropical and temperature climates, as well as being very versatile foods, their cultivation and adoption into varying cuisines spread rapidly through many parts of the world.

They have become a staple in central Europe where they are dried for paprika, an essential flavour in Louisiana Creole dishes, and an integral ingredient in Mexican and Portuguese cuisines. Currently, the main producers of capsicum are China, Turkey, Spain, Romania, Nigeria and Mexico.

One cup of raw, chopped red peppers provides over 100 per cent of the recommended daily value for vitamins C and A, through its concentration of carotenoids such as beta-carotene. These antioxidants work together to effectively neutralise free radicals, which can travel through the body causing huge amounts of damage to cells. Free radicals are major players in the build-up of cholesterol in the arteries that leads to atherosclerosis and heart disease; the nerve and blood vessel damage seen in diabetes; the cloudy lenses of cataracts; the joint pain and damage seen in osteoarthritis and rheumatoid arthritis; and the wheezing and airway tightening of asthma. By providing these two potent destroyers of free radicals, bell peppers may help prevent or reduce some of the symptoms of these conditions by shutting down the source of the problem.

Red peppers are also an excellent source of vitamin B6. Green peppers are rich in fibre, folate, vitamin K, molybdenum and manganese. In addition to beta-carotene, red peppers contain the beneficial phyto-nutrients lycopene, lutein and zeaxanthin.

Bell peppers are one of the best vegetables to serve in a crudité platter not only because they add a brilliant splash of colour, but their texture is the perfect crunchy complement for dips.

Cauliflower (phool gobi): Cauliflower, *Brassica oleracea botrytis*, traces its ancestry to the wild cabbage, a plant thought to have originated in ancient Asia Minor. The United States, France, Italy, India and China produce significant amounts of cauliflower.

Consumption of cruciferous vegetables, such as cauliflower, is known to reduce the risk of several cancers, especially lung, colon, breast, ovarian and bladder cancer. Certain compounds present in these vegetables appear to stop enzymes from activating cancer-causing agents in the body, and they increase the activity of enzymes that disable and eliminate carcinogens.

One cup of boiled cauliflower is an excellent source of vitamin C (91.5 per cent of the daily value), folate (13.6 per cent), and dietary fibre (13.4 per cent). That same amount of cauliflower also serves as a very good source of vitamins B5 and B6, manganese and omega-3 fatty acids.

Cauliflower contains phyto-nutrients that release odorous sulphur compounds when heated. These odours become stronger with increased cooking time. To minimise odour, retain the vegetable's crisp texture and reduce nutrient loss, cauliflower should be cooked for a very short while. The florets are the part of the plant that most people eat. However, the stem and leaves are edible too and are especially good for adding to soup stocks.

Cucumber (kheera/kakdi): To be as 'cool as a cucumber' add them to your menu during the warm summer months when they are in season. This vegetable's high water content gives it a unique moist and cooling taste. Cucumbers are scientifically called *Cucumis sativus* and belong to the same family as watermelon, zucchini, pumpkin and other types of squash.

Cucumbers are believed to have originated over 10,000 years ago in southern Asia. Early explorers and travellers introduced this vegetable to India and other parts of Asia. It was very popular in the ancient civilisations of Egypt, Greece and Rome, whose people used it not only as a food but also for its beneficial skin-healing properties.

Cucumbers are a very good source of vitamin C and molybdenum. They are also a good source of vitamin A, potassium, manganese, folate, dietary fibre and magnesium, and contain the important mineral silica. The cucumber flesh is primarily composed of water but also contains ascorbic acid (vitamin C) and caffeic acid, both of which help soothe skin irritations and reduce swellings. The cucumber's hard skin is rich in fibre and contains a variety of beneficial minerals including silica, potassium and magnesium.

The silica in cucumber is an essential component of healthy connective tissue — muscles, tendons, ligaments, cartilage and bone. The juice is often recommended as a source of silica to improve the complexion and health of the skin; plus its high water content makes it naturally hydrating — a must for glowing skin. Cucumber is also used topically for various types of skin problems, including swelling under the eyes and sunburn.

Adding a crunchy cool cucumber to your salads is an especially good way to increase your fibre intake because it comes naturally pre-packaged with the extra fluid you need when consuming more fibre.

Fenugreek (methi): The name fenugreek is from the Latin name foenum-graecum or 'Greek hay'. In India, fenugreek seeds are mixed with yogurt and used as a conditioner for hair.

Fenugreek belongs to the Leguminosae family and its botanical name is *Trigonella foenum-graecum*. It is called by different names in different parts of India: menthya in Kannada, ventayan and uluva in Malayalam, vendayam and venthiyam in Tamil and menthulu and mentulu in Telugu. It is called methi in Hindi, Bengali, Gujarati, Maharashtrian, Oriya, Punjabi, Sanskrit and Urdu.

It is grown as a herb (the leaves) and a spice (the seeds) in India. Both the plant and the seed are considered to have immense medicinal values. The leaf is eaten as salad and cooked as a vegetable, popularly known as methi saag. It is a winter crop and is fairly tolerant to frost and very low temperatures. It is best suited to tracts of moderate to low rainfall and is sown in all types of soil but perform better in loam and clayey loam, with proper drainage. It can also be grown on black cotton soils. In a nutshell, fenugreek seeds contain many substances like protein, starch, sugars, mucilage, mineral matters, volatile oil, fixed oil, vitamins and enzymes, and are rich in essential amino acids.

Fresh tender pods, leaves and shoots, a good source of iron, calcium, protein, vitamins A and C, are cooked as curried vegetables from ancient times in India, Egypt and other countries. As a spice, fenugreek adds to the nutritive value and flavour of foods. Because of this, it is of considerable importance in those countries in the Middle and Far East where vegetarian diets are customary for cultural and religious reasons. Fenugreek's main importance is as one of the principal odorous constituents of curry powder.

Apart from culinary use, fenugreek has been used in medicine since ancient times in India. The traditional uses of fenugreek include bronchial problems, tuberculosis, gout, general body pain, swollen glands, skin problems, low libido, wounds and abscesses, arthritis and digestive problems. Although the use of most spices in medicine has declined considerably in recent years, fenugreek is an exception to the rule. Recent studies in England indicate that fenugreek seeds contain a substantial amount of the steroidal substance diosgenin, which is used as a starting material in the synthesis of sex hormones and oral contraceptives. The seed is used by Indian women to promote lactation. Ground fine and mixed with cottonseed, it is fed to cows to increase milk flow. It is used as a conditioning powder to produce a glossy coat on horses.

Mushroom (dhingri): Mushrooms come in numerous varieties, each with its own characteristics and qualities. While often thought of as a vegetable and prepared like one, mushrooms are actually fungi, a special type of living organism that has no roots, leaves, flowers or seeds. There are three different types of button mushrooms — white, crimini and Portobello. The white mushroom is the most common variety and is the cream coloured one that often adorns salads.

The crimini mushroom, which looks just like the white one but is coffee coloured, actually has a more distinctive flavour. The Portobello mushroom, whose large size and meaty flavour make it a wonderful vegetarian entrée, is actually an overgrown crimini mushroom. The scientific name for these mushrooms is *Agaricus bisporus*. Button mushrooms have grown wild since prehistoric times, having been consumed as food by the early hunter-gatherers.

Since ancient times, mushrooms have been thought to have special powers. The Egyptians believed that they granted immortality, and since only the pharaohs were supposed to be worthy of this gift, the common people were not even allowed to touch mushrooms, let alone eat them.

Crimini mushrooms are an excellent source of several minerals including selenium, copper, potassium, phosphorus, manganese and zinc, and of B vitamins including B2, pantothenic acid, niacin, B1, B6, as well as protein. Zinc affects many fundamental processes, perhaps the most important of which is its immune function. The B vitamin, pantothenic acid, plays an important role in the prevention of fatigue since it supports the functioning of the adrenal glands, particularly in times of stress.

A symbol of longevity because of their health-promoting properties, shiitake mushrooms have been used medicinally by the Chinese for over 6,000 years. They have brown, slightly convex caps that range in diameter from 2 to 4 inches. The scientific name for shiitake mushroom is *Lentinus edodes*. They are an excellent source of selenium and a very good source of iron, protein, dietary fibre and vitamin C.

Mushrooms are porous, so if they are exposed to too much water they will quickly absorb it and become soggy. Therefore, the best way to clean mushrooms without sacrificing their texture and taste is to clean them using minimal, if any, water. To do this, simply wipe them with a slightly damp paper towel or kitchen cloth.

The best way to store mushrooms is in the refrigerator, either wrapped in a damp cloth and put in a loosely-closed paper bag, or laid out in a glass dish that is covered with a damp cloth. These methods help preserve their moisture without making them soggy and will keep them fresh for several days.

Mustard greens (sarson): Mustard greens are the leaves of the mustard plant, *Brassica juncea*. They can have a crumpled or flat texture and toothed, scalloped, frilled or lacy edges. Mustard greens originated in the Himalayan region of India and have been grown and consumed for over 5,000 years. They are notable in many different cuisines, ranging from Chinese to southern American. Like turnip greens, they may have become an integral part of southern American cuisine during the slavery era, serving as a substitute for the greens that were an essential part of western African food. Mustard greens are an excellent source of many vitamins including vitamins A, B6, folate and vitamins C and E. It also provides calcium, magnesium, manganese and dietary fibre. The vitamin E supplied by mustard greens is instrumental in a host of different mechanisms that reduce the development of atherosclerosis and protecting LDL (the bad cholesterol) particles from oxidation. Vitamin B6 in mustard has been shown to decrease platelet clumping, thereby reducing the risk of thrombosis (clot formation).

Since magnesium is necessary for normal blood vessel tone and function, mustard greens may also be good for women undergoing menopause. They provide nutrients that are supportive of bone health, as a higher intake of calcium can help to prevent bone loss that usually occurs at this stage of life. Women with osteoporosis also have low bone magnesium content and other signs of magnesium deficiency, so mustard greens would once again be helpful.

Vitamin C works to neutralise free radicals that are responsible for causing smooth muscle contraction and airway constriction in asthma. Additionally, it assists with the breakdown of histamine, one of the inflammatory chemicals that are overproduced in asthma and many other immune-related disorders.

The easiest way to clean mustard greens or any other greens, for that matter, is to place them in a large bowl of tepid water and swirl them around with your hands. This will dislodge sand and dirt. Wait for a while to let the dirt sink. Remove the greens from the water, empty the bowl, refill with clean water and repeat this process until no sand or dirt remains in the water (usually two to three times will do the trick).

Okra (bhindi): Okra, *Abelmoschus esculentus*, known by many other names such as bhindi in Hindi or lady fingers in several other countries, is a flowering plant of the mallow family along with such species as cotton, cocoa and hibiscus, valued for its edible green fruits.

The species apparently originated in the Ethiopian highlands, though the manner of distribution from there is undocumented. The Egyptians and Moors of the twelfth and thirteenth centuries used the Arab word for the plant, suggesting that it had come from the east.

This food is low in saturated fat, and very low in cholesterol and sodium. It is a good source of protein, niacin, iron, phosphorus, zinc and copper, and a very good source of dietary fibre, vitamins A, C and K, thiamin, riboflavin, folate, calcium, magnesium, potassium and manganese.

Potato (alu): Potatoes, *Solanum tuberosum*, originated in the Andean mountain region of South America. Researchers estimate that potatoes have been cultivated by the Indians living in these areas for between 4,000 and 7,000 years. Unlike many other foods, potatoes could be grown at the high altitudes typical of this area and therefore became a staple food for these hardy people. Potatoes are one of the vegetables in the nightshade (Solanaceae) family, which includes aubergines, tomatoes and bell peppers. They should not be stored in the refrigerator, as their starch content turns to sugar, giving them an undesirable taste. In addition, they should not be stored near onions, as the gases that each emits causes the degradation of the other. Wherever you store them, they should be kept in a paper bag.

Potatoes are a very good source of vitamin C. They are also rich in vitamin B6, copper, potassium, manganese and dietary fibre. They contain a variety of phyto-nutrients that have antioxidant properties. Among the important health-promoting compounds are carotenoids, flavonoids and caffeic acid, as well as unique tuber storage proteins, such as patatin, which exhibits activity against free radicals.

....

Radish (mooli): The radish, *Raphanus sativus*, is an edible root vegetable of the Brassicaceae family that was domesticated in Europe in pre-Roman times. The descriptive Greek name of the genus Raphanus means 'quickly appearing' and refers to the rapid germination of these plants. Raphanistrum, from the same Greek root, is an old name once used for this genus. They are grown and consumed throughout the world. There are numerous varieties of radishes, varying in size, colour and duration for cultivation.

Radishes and their greens provide an excellent source of vitamin C. The leaves contain almost six times the vitamin C content of the root and are a good source of calcium. Radishes, like other members of the cruciferous family (cabbage, kale, broccoli, Brussels sprouts), contain cancer-protective properties. Throughout history, radishes have been effective when used as a medicinal food for liver disorders. They contain a variety of sulphur-based chemicals that increase bile flow. Therefore, they help to maintain a healthy gall bladder and liver, and improve digestion. Fresh radish roots contain a larger amount of vitamin C than the cooked ones.

....

Spinach (palak): Spinach, *Spinacia oleracea*, belongs to the Amaranthaceae family. It is native to Central and south-western Asia and is thought to have originated in ancient Persia (Iran). It made its way to China in the seventh century when the king of Nepal sent it as a gift to that country. It grows well in temperate climates. Spinach should be washed well, as described for mustard greens, since the leaves and stems tend to collect sand and soil. It is considered a rich source of iron and calcium. The iron in spinach is poorly absorbed by the body unless eaten with vitamin C. The type of iron found in spinach is non-blood (non-heme); it is a plant iron, which the body does not absorb as efficiently as blood (heme) iron, found in meat. Spinach has high nutritional value and is extremely rich in antioxidants, especially when fresh, steamed, or quickly boiled. It is a rich source of vitamins A (and lutein), B2, B6, C, E and K, magnesium, manganese, folate, iron, calcium, potassium, folic acid, copper, protein, phosphorus, zinc, niacin, selenium and omega-3 fatty acids. Researchers have identified at least 13 different flavonoid compounds in spinach that function as antioxidants and anti-cancer agents. The vitamin K provided by spinach — almost 200 per cent of the daily value in one cup of fresh spinach leaves and over 1,000 per cent in one cup of boiled spinach (which contains about six times as much spinach) — is important for maintaining bone health. Vitamin K1 helps prevent excessive activation of osteoclasts, the cells that break down bone. Additionally, friendly bacteria in our intestines convert vitamin K1 into K2, which activates osteocalcin, the major non-collagen protein in bone. The calcium and magnesium found in spinach are other bone-building nutrients. Lutein, a carotenoid protecting against eye diseases such as age-related macular degeneration and cataract, is found in green vegetables, especially spinach, as well as kale and broccoli.

Yam (suran): This vegetable belongs to the Dioscoreaceae family. It has a rough skin which is difficult to peel, but which softens on heating. The skin colour varies from dark brown to light pink. The vegetable is composed of a soft flesh called the 'meat', which could be white, yellow, purple or pink in ripe yams. Yams are a primary agricultural commodity in West Africa and New Guinea. They were first cultivated in Africa and Asia around 8,000 BC. Due to their abundance and consequently, their importance to survival, the yam was highly regarded in Nigerian ceremonial culture and even worshipped. Yams are still important for survival in these regions. The tubers can be stored for up to six months without refrigeration, which makes them a valuable resource during food scarcity at the beginning of the wet season.

Yam is an important food component of the Konyak tribal people (Northeast India), where it is consumed throughout the year in various preparations after preserving it. As the people practised slash-and-burn cultivation, the rice produced was never enough to feed the family throughout the year. Yam was used to supplement rice to keep the family surviving, fit and healthy. It is harvested, cut and dried for preservation. The leaves are also preserved by drying.

Yams are a good source of vitamin B6, which is needed by the body to break down a substance called homocysteine, which can directly damage blood vessel walls. They are a good source of potassium, a mineral that helps to control blood pressure. Wild yam also has a history of traditional use in herbal medicine, especially Chinese herbal medicine, to affect organ system function, particular kidney function. Wild (Chinese) yam has also been used to support the female endocrine system.

Breakfast

Bhajil Poha (Crisp-Fried Beaten Rice)

6 servings

½ tsp cumin seeds/jeera
1 tsp coriander seeds/dhania
3 tbsp ghee
4 cups beaten rice/poha
1 cup grated fresh coconut
3 green chillies, chopped
1 tbsp sugar
1 tsp salt

Roast the cumin and coriander seeds on a dry tava or griddle and powder them coarsely. Set aside.

Put the ghee in a large kadhai or wok over low heat. When hot, roast the beaten rice in the ghee till crisp, tossing continuously to prevent it from burning. Remove from heat.

Mix the powdered spices, coconut, green chillies, sugar and salt in a bowl.

Add the roasted rice and toss till the ingredients are well mixed.

Serve before the rice gets soft.

Poha Pachadi (Beaten Rice and Coconut Relish)

About 4 servings

2-3 green chillies, chopped
1 tsp salt
2 tsp coriander seeds/dhania
1 tsp cumin seeds/jeera
2" piece jaggery/gud, grated
1 cup grated fresh coconut
1 cup beaten rice/poha

Tempering
3 tsp oil
½ tsp mustard seeds/rai/
  sarson
3-4 curry leaves

Grind the green chillies and salt together. Add the coriander seeds, cumin seeds and jaggery and grind again. Mix in the coconut and grind some more.

Transfer the ground ingredients to a bowl. Gently mix in the beaten rice.

Put the oil in a small pan over moderate heat. When hot, add the mustard seeds and curry leaves. When the mustard seeds splutter, pour the tempering over the rice mixture.

Toss well and serve.

Kanchipuram Idli (Kanchipuram Steamed Rice Cakes)

Makes about 16 idlis

1 cup rice
1 cup husked
   black gram/urad dal
1 tbsp husked
   Bengal gram/chana dal
½ cup grated fresh coconut
2 tbsp oil + extra
   for greasing idli mould
4 green chillies, chopped
½ tsp coarsely ground
   black pepper/kali miri
8 cashew nuts, quartered
1" piece ginger, chopped
5-6 curry leaves, chopped
¼ tsp sodium bicarbonate
1¼ tsp salt
¾ cup sour yogurt/dahi

Wash the rice and black gram and soak them together in water for 2-3 hours.

Drain the rice and black gram and grind to make a light, frothy batter, gradually adding about 4 tbsp of water.

Transfer the batter to a bowl, cover and set aside to ferment for 8-10 hours.

Wash the Bengal gram and soak it in water for 30 minutes. Drain, add it to the idli batter with the coconut and mix well.

Put 2 tbsp of oil in a small frying pan over moderate heat. When hot, add the green chillies, pepper, cashew nuts and ginger and sauté lightly.

Pour the contents of the pan into the batter, which should have a thick, semi-solid consistency.

Mix in the curry leaves, sodium bicarbonate, salt and yogurt.

Grease the depressions of an idli mould with oil and fill them with the batter.

Steam the idli in batches, in a pressure cooker without the weight on for 20 minutes each.

Serve immediately.

Idiappam (Rice String Hoppers)

About 8 servings

3 cups rice
2 cups freshly grated tender
   coconut
1½ tsp salt
Oil for greasing pan and idli
   mould
A piece of banana leaf

Wash the rice and soak it in water for 3 hours.

Drain the rice and grind it with the coconut to make a fine batter, gradually adding about 6 tbsp of water. Mix in the salt.

Lightly grease a pan with oil. Transfer the batter to the pan. Stir in 3-4 cups of water.

Place the pan over moderate heat and cook, stirring continuously for about 15 minutes, till the batter is stiff enough to shape into balls.

Remove from heat and allow it to cool a little. Grease an idli mould with a little oil.

Shape the batter into large lemon-sized ovals, while still warm. Make a small depression in each ball with a moistened finger.

Spread the banana leaf on the perforated sheet of the idli mould and arrange the balls on it. Steam them in batches in a pressure cooker without the weight on for 15 minutes each, till cooked. Remove the balls from the cooker.

Insert one ball at a time in a semia mould while still hot. Press the ball and collect the emerging strands of idiappam on a plate placed underneath.

Notes

The idiappam can be dried in the sun and stored in an airtight container for up to 6 months. Use it to make idiappam upma (page 26).

Spread a clean damp cloth on a wooden board and lay the strands on it without allowing them to touch each other.

When cool, transfer the idiappam to a bowl and set aside covered with cloth.

Serve with any chutney of choice (pages 143-144).

Idiappam Upma (Rice String Hopper Pilaf)

About 8 servings

3-4 tbsp sun-dried idiappam
(page 25)
½ tsp salt
1 tsp sugar

Tempering
2 tsp ghee
½ tsp mustard seeds/rai/
sarson
¼ tsp cumin seeds/jeera
½ tsp husked black gram/
urad dal
3-4 green chillies, slit
8-10 curry leaves

Garnish
½ cup grated fresh coconut

Soak the dried idiappam in water for 6-8 hours, till soft. Rinse, drain and set aside.

Put the ghee for tempering in a large frying pan over moderate heat. When hot, add the remaining tempering ingredients. When the mustard seeds splutter, add the idiappam.

Sprinkle in the salt and sugar and mix gently.

Cover the pan and cook over low heat for about 5 minutes.

Garnish with coconut and serve immediately.

Panpolo/Neer Dosai (Coconut Rice Pancakes)

Makes 18-20 dosai

2 cups rice
1 cup grated fresh coconut
1 tsp salt
Oil for frying

Wash the rice and soak in water for 2-3 hours.

Drain the rice and grind it with the coconut to make a fine batter, gradually adding about 4 tbsp of water.

Add the salt and give it a whirl before transferring the batter to a bowl.

Mix in about 2 cups of water to make a batter of pouring consistency.

Brush a dosai pan lightly with oil and place it over moderate heat. Spread a ladle of batter thinly in the pan, tilting it till it covers the base.

Cook the dosai on one side only, till the base is crisp, the edges are lacy and the centre is still soft and spongy.

Fold it in half and serve immediately with any chutney of choice (pages 143-144), butter or jaggery syrup.

Make the remaining dosai in the same way.

Musti Dosai (Fenugreek Rice Pancakes)

Makes 12-15 dosai

2 cups rice
3 tbsp husked black gram/
   urad dal
1 tbsp fenugreek seeds/methi
1 cup beaten rice/poha
½ cup grated fresh coconut
1 tsp salt
Oil for frying

Wash the rice and gram and soak them in water with the fenugreek seeds for 2 hours.

Rinse the beaten rice and soak it separately for 30 minutes.

Drain the rice, gram and fenugreek seeds and grind them with the coconut to make a coarse batter, gradually adding about 4 tbsp of water.

Drain the beaten rice, add it to the grinder and grind to make a smooth batter of a semi-liquid consistency.

Sprinkle in the salt and mix well.

Transfer the batter to a bowl, cover and let it ferment overnight.

The next day, prepare dosai as given for panpolo/neer dosai (page 27), cooking them on one side only, but add a little more batter to the pan to make a slightly thicker dosai.

Masala Dosai (Rice Pancakes with a Potato Filling)

Makes 12-15 dosa

Dosai Batter
1 cup uncooked rice
¾ cup husked black gram/
  urad dal
1 cup cooked white rice
2 tsp salt
Ghee for frying

Potato filling
3 tbsp oil
2" piece ginger, sliced
3 small green chillies, slit
3 small onions, sliced
2 tsp turmeric powder/haldi
1½ tsp salt
500 gms potatoes, boiled,
  peeled and coarsely
  crumbled

Dosai batter
Wash the uncooked rice and gram and soak in water with the cooked rice for 5-6 hours.

Drain the rice and gram and grind it with the cooked rice to make a smooth batter, gradually adding about 3 tbsp of water. Sprinkle in the salt and mix well.

Transfer the batter to a bowl, cover and let it ferment overnight.

Potato filling
Put the oil in a pan over moderate heat. When hot, add the ginger and green chillies.

Give it a stir and add the onions. Fry till they are golden brown.

Sprinkle in the turmeric powder and salt. Mix well. Add the potatoes and toss gently till well coated.

To cook and assemble the dosai
Brush a dosai pan with ghee and place it over moderate heat. When hot, spread a ladle of batter thinly in the pan, tilting it till it covers the base. Cover the pan and cook the dosai till the base is crisp and golden.

Uncover the pan and spread some potato filling along one half of the dosai. Fold the other half over it.

Cook for a few minutes more and serve immediately with sambar (page 47) and any chutney of choice (pages 143-144).

Make the remaining dosai in the same way.

Oothappa (Rice and Black Gram Pancakes)

Makes 8-10 oothappa

2 cups rice
1 cup husked black gram/
    urad dal
1½ tsp salt
4 green chillies, chopped
4 medium onions, chopped
1" piece ginger, chopped
2 tbsp chopped coriander
    leaves/hara dhania
Oil for frying

Wash the rice and gram and soak them separately in water for 2-3 hours.

Drain the gram and grind it to make a fine, frothy batter, gradually adding about 2 tbsp of water. Transfer to a bowl and set aside.

Drain the rice and grind it to make a slightly coarse batter, gradually adding about 4 tbsp of water. Add the salt and mix the rice batter with the gram batter. It should be moderately thick, like a cake batter.

Cover and set aside to ferment overnight.

The next day, combine the chopped ingredients in a bowl and set aside.

Brush a dosai pan with oil and put it over moderate heat. When hot, spread a large ladle of batter thickly and evenly in the pan, tilting it till it covers the base. Cover the pan and cook for about 3-4 minutes, till the base is golden brown.

Open the pan and sprinkle some of the onion mix over the oothappa. Gently turn it over.

Lift the oothappa from the pan, after the other side is just cooked and set. Flip over on to a plate and serve at once.

Make the remaining oothappa in the same way.

Paan Patholi (Steamed Turmeric Rice Dumplings)

Makes 12-16 patholi

1 cup uncooked rice
2 cups grated fresh coconut
1 cup puffed rice/murmura
A pinch of salt
1 cup grated jaggery/gud
1/3 cup powdered popped
   rice/kurmura
2 green cardamoms/
   chhoti elaichi
50 turmeric leaves/haldi paan

Wash the uncooked rice and soak it in water for 1 hour.

Drain the rice and grind it with 2 tbsp of coconut, till fairly smooth, gradually adding about 2 tbsp of water. Add the puffed rice and grind to make a fine batter.

Sprinkle in the salt and 1 tbsp of jaggery and grind for another 2 minutes. Transfer to a bowl and set aside.

Combine the remaining coconut and jaggery with the powdered popped rice and cardamom in a bowl.

Spread about 2 tsp of the batter thinly on each turmeric leaf. Place a small quantity of the coconut-jaggery mix over the batter. Fold each leaf lengthwise to form a patholi.

Place the patholi, side by side, on the perforated sheet of an idli mould.

Steam the patholi in batches in a pressure cooker without the weight on for 15-20 minutes, till cooked.

Remove the patholi from the cooker. When cool, extract them from the leaves.

Serve with ghee or honey.

Ragi Idli (Steamed Finger Millet Cakes)

Makes 30-40 idlis

2 cups rice
1 cup husked black gram/
  urad dal
1 cup finger millet flour/ragi/
  nachni ka atta
2 tsp salt
Oil for greasing idli mould

Wash the rice and gram and soak them separately overnight in water.

Drain the rice and grind it to make a slightly coarse batter, gradually adding about 4 tbsp of water.

Drain the gram and grind it to make a fine, frothy batter, gradually adding about 2 tbsp of water.

Mix the rice and the gram batters in a bowl and sift in the millet flour and salt. Mix well and set aside for 5-6 hours to ferment.

Grease the depressions of an idli mould with oil and fill them with the batter.

Steam the idli in batches in a pressure cooker, without the weight on for 10 minutes, till cooked.

Remove the idli from the cooker and serve hot with sambar (page 47) and any chutney of choice (pages 143-144).

High-Protein Breakfast Cereal

About 20 servings

¾ cup amaranth flour/
   ramdana ka atta
2½ cups rolled oats/jai
½ cup chopped walnuts
½ cup grated fresh coconut
1/3 cup pumpkin seeds
1/3 cup peanuts
1 tsp cinnamon powder/
   dalchini
½ cup oil
½ cup honey
1 tsp vanilla extract (optional)
¾ cup seedless raisins or
   other dried fruits (optional)

Sift the flour into a large bowl. Mix in the oats, walnuts, coconut, pumpkin seeds, peanuts and cinnamon.

Put the oil and honey in a pan over low heat and stir till well blended. Mix in the vanilla (if used).

Pour the contents of the pan into the oat mix. Stir gently till the dry ingredients are well coated.

Spread the mix in a thin layer on a baking tray.

Bake in an oven preheated to 150°C for 20-30 minutes, stirring every 10 minutes, till it is golden brown.

Remove from the oven and allow it to cool. Stir in the raisins or other dried fruits (if used).

Store in the refrigerator in an airtight container.

Variation: Add ½ cup of mashed table bananas or your favourite fruit, puréed, to the honey and oil while it is being heated.

Notes

This delicious mix makes a quick, high-energy breakfast, rich in proteins, calcium and iron, especially suited to school- and college-goers and working people. It is also much cheaper than buying fortified breakfast cereals.

Kulthi ka Dal Idli (Steamed Horse Gram Cakes)

Makes 20-25 idli

1 cup horse gram/kulthi ka
  dal/gahath
1 cup husked black gram/
  urad dal
1½ cups rice
3 tsp salt
Oil for greasing idli mould

Wash the horse gram and black gram and soak them together in water for 2 hours. Wash the rice and soak it separately in water for 2 hours.

Drain the horse gram and black gram and grind them to make a fine, frothy batter, gradually adding about 4 tbsp of water. Set aside in a bowl.

Drain the rice and grind it to a coarse batter, gradually adding about 3 tbsp of water.

Mix the rice batter into the gram batter. It should have a thick, semi-solid consistency. Sprinkle in the salt and mix well.

Grease the depressions of an idli mould with oil and fill them with the batter.

Steam the idli in batches, in a pressure cooker without the weight on for 30 minutes, till cooked.

Remove the mould from the cooker.

Cut idli into slices and serve immediately.

Alu Paratha (Pan-Fried Flatbread with a Potato Filling)

Makes 8 paratha

2 cups wholewheat flour/
  gehun ka atta + extra for
  rolling
1 tsp salt
2 tsp ghee

Filling
1 tbsp grated fresh coconut
1 tsp salt
6 green chillies, finely
  chopped
2 tbsp finely chopped
  coriander leaves/
  hara dhania
A pinch of asafoetida powder/
  hing, dissolved in
  1 tsp water
5 medium potatoes, boiled
  peeled and mashed

Sift the flour and salt into a bowl. Gradually add about 1 cup of hot water and knead to prepare a soft, pliable dough. Set aside.

Mix the coconut with the salt, green chillies, coriander leaves and asafoetida water in a bowl.

Add the mashed potatoes and mix till well blended.

Divide the filling and dough into 8 portions.

Roll out a portion of dough on a lightly floured surface into a roti. Place a portion of potato mix on the roti. Fold the dough over the filling to cover it completely and press the top to seal, using a little water if required.

Dust with flour and roll into a 6" round paratha.

Make the remaining parathas in the same way.

Roast each paratha on a heated tava or griddle lightly smeared with ghee, over moderate heat for 2 minutes, till brown spots appear on the surface. Flip over and roast for another 2 minutes.

Serve hot.

Mooli Paratha (Pan-Fried Flatbread with White Radish)

Makes 12-16 paratha

4 cups wholewheat flour/
   gehun ka atta + extra for
   rolling
1½ cups grated white radish/
   mooli
2 tsp salt
2 tsp cumin powder/jeera
2 tsp red chilli powder
2 tbsp oil
Ghee for roasting paratha

Sift the flour into a bowl. Mix in the remaining ingredients, except the oil and ghee. Knead to prepare a soft, pliable dough, adding a little water if necessary.

Add the oil and knead to make the dough softer and more pliable. Set aside for 1 hour.

Divide the dough into 12-16 portions and roll each portion on a lightly floured surface to make 6" round paratha.

Roast each paratha on a heated tava or griddle, lightly smeared with ghee, over moderate heat for 2 minutes, till brown spots appear on the surface. Flip over and roast for another 2 minutes. Serve hot.

Thalipeeth (Mixed Flour Pan-Fried Flatbread)

Makes about 25 thalipeeth

- 4 cups rice flour/chaval ka atta
- 2 cups sorghum flour/jowar ka atta
- ½ cup gram flour/besan
- ½ cup wholewheat flour/ gehun ka atta
- 2 tsp cumin powder/jeera
- 1 tsp sesame seeds/til
- 4 tbsp red chilli powder
- 3 tsp salt
- A piece of banana leaf or a thick polythene sheet
- Oil for cooking thalipeeth

Sift all the flours into a bowl. Mix in the remaining ingredients, except the banana leaf and oil. Gradually add 2-2½ cups of water and knead to prepare a soft, pliable dough.

Pinch off lime-sized balls of dough. Flatten each portion on a moist banana leaf or polythene sheet, into a ¼" thick, 4"-5" round roti.

Put a tava or griddle over low heat and brush with a little oil. When hot, transfer a thalipeeth carefully to the tava or griddle. Drizzle a little oil around the sides and cook over low heat for 1 minute.

Turn the thalipeeth over and cook for another minute, till crisp and golden brown. Serve hot.

Variation: You can also deep-fry the thalipeeth.

Methi Thepla (Fenugreek-Flavoured Flat Bread)

Makes 6 thepla

1 cup wholewheat flour/gehun
   ka atta + extra for rolling
2 green chillies, crushed
1 tsp red chilli powder
½ tsp turmeric powder/haldi
1 tbsp ginger-garlic paste
1 tsp ajwain
A pinch of asafoetida powder/
   hing
½ cup chopped fenugreek
   leaves/methi
1 tsp coriander powder/
   dhania
1 tsp cumin powder/jeera
¾ tsp salt
Oil for cooking thepla

Sift the flour into a shallow bowl. Add the remaining ingredients, except the oil. Mix and add 1 tsp oil.

Knead for about 5 minutes. Set aside for about 15 minutes.

Divide the dough into 6 even-sized balls. Roll them on a lightly floured surface into 5" round thepla.

Put a tava or griddle, lightly smeared with oil, over low heat. When hot, place a thepla on it.

Roast for about 1 minute, till brown spots appear on the base. Smear with oil, flip over and roast the other side for another minute.

Serve hot with butter, yogurt or any chutney of choice (pages 143-144).

Kakdi Doddak (Cucumber Bread)

Makes 8 doddak

1 small cucumber (4"-5" long)
½ cup wholewheat flour/ gehun ka atta + extra for rolling
1½ cups coarsely ground rice/ rice rava
3 tbsp grated fresh coconut
½" piece ginger, finely chopped
6 green chillies, finely chopped
A sprig of curry leaves
4 tsp sugar
1 tsp salt
Oil for greasing pan

Peel the cucumber. Remove the seeds and discard them. Grate the cucumber flesh into a small bowl.

Sift the flour into another bowl. Add the cucumber, ground rice, coconut, ginger, green chillies, curry leaves, sugar and salt and mix till the ingredients can be gathered up into a ball of dough. Add a little water if necessary.

Knead the dough gently on a lightly floured surface, for a minute or so.

Brush a frying pan with oil and put it over low heat. When hot, pinch off about 2 tbsp of dough and use your fingers to flatten it on the pan into a 4" doddak. Roast on both sides for about 2 minutes each, till light brown.

Make the remaining doddak in the same way.

Serve hot.

Dalia Upma (Broken Wheat Pilaf)

4 servings

½ cup broken wheat/dalia or wheat germ
½ cup broken sorghum/jowar or pearl millet/bajra grains
1 medium onion, finely chopped
1 medium tomato, finely chopped
1 tbsp toasted white rolled oats/jai
A pinch of turmeric powder/haldi
1 tsp salt
1 tbsp coriander leaves/hara dhania, finely chopped
1 lime, juice extracted

Tempering
1 tbsp oil
½ tsp mustard seeds/rai/sarson
½ tsp cumin seeds/jeera
4-5 curry leaves
2 green chillies, finely chopped
4-5 cashew nuts, broken
A pinch of asafoetida powder/hing

Roast the broken wheat and sorghum or millet in a dry, heavy-based pan over moderate heat stirring continuously for about 2 minutes. Remove from heat and allow it to cool.

Pressure-cook the roasted wheat and sorghum or millet with 2 cups of water for 5-7 minutes after the cooker reaches full pressure. Open the cooker when cool.

Put the oil for tempering in a pan over moderate heat. When hot, add the remaining tempering ingredients. When the mustard seeds splutter, add the onion and tomato and stir-fry for about 2 minutes.

Drain the broken wheat and sorghum or millet and add them to the pan with the remaining ingredients.

Cover the pan and cook over low heat, till the upma is fluffy and dry.

Serve hot.

Main Course
Dal and Vegetable Dishes

Dal, Bati Churma (Sweetened Lentils with Baked Dumplings)

6 servings

This is one of the most popular dishes in Rajasthani cuisine. It is made with dal, bati which are baked wheat balls, and churma which is coarsely ground wheat, crushed and cooked with ghee and sugar. Churma is traditionally made by mashing wheat flour bati or leftover roti with ghee and jaggery.

Bati
2 cups slightly coarse
  wholewheat flour/
  gehun ka atta
1 tsp ajwain
1 tsp cumin seeds/jeera
½ tsp sugar
1½ tsp salt
1 tbsp + 2 tbsp ghee

Dal
1 cup pigeon peas/tuvar dal/
  arhar dal
1 tsp red chilli powder
1 tsp turmeric powder/haldi
½ tsp coriander powder/
  dhania
1 tsp salt

Tempering
2 tbsp ghee
½ tsp mustard seeds/rai/
  sarson
½ tsp cumin seeds/jeera
½" piece ginger, crushed
8-10 curry leaves
3-4 green chillies, slit
1 medium tomato, finely
  chopped
¼ tsp asafoetida powder/hing

Bati
Sift the flour into a bowl. Add the remaining bati ingredients, except the ghee. Mix in 1 tbsp of ghee. Gradually add about 1 cup of water and knead to prepare a very stiff dough. Cover and set aside for 1 hour. Knead till smooth.

Pinch off golf-ball-sized balls of dough and shape into round bati.

Place the bati on a baking tray and bake in an oven preheated to 230°C for 8-10 minutes till semi-baked.

Put 2 tbsp of ghee in a kadhai or wok over low heat. When hot, add the bati. Cover the pan and cook for 8-10 minutes, tossing frequently, till light brown. Remove from heat and set aside.

Dal
Wash the dal and pressure-cook it with 2 cups of water for 15 minutes after the cooker reaches full pressure. Allow the dal to cool slightly and whisk till smooth, adding a little water if necessary. Set aside.

Put the ghee for tempering in a pan over moderate heat. When hot, add the mustard and cumin seeds. When they splutter, add the remaining tempering ingredients. Stir for a minute.

Sprinkle in the spice powders and a few drops of water. Stir for 2-3 minutes and add the salt and dal. Set aside.

Churma
2 cups wholewheat flour/
    gehun ka atta
1½ cups ghee
¼ cup crumbled khoya/mawa
    (unsweetened milk solids)
4 green cardamoms/chhoti
    elaichi
1" stick cinnamon/dalchini
¾ cup sugar, crushed
¼ cup almonds blanched,
    peeled and finely chopped

Garnish
1 tbsp finely chopped
    coriander leaves/
    hara dhania

Churma

Sift the flour into a bowl. Melt $1/3$ cup of the measured ghee and mix it into the flour. Gradually add about $1/3$ cup of water and knead to prepare a stiff dough.

Divide the dough into 15-20 balls.

Heat the remaining ghee in a kadhai or wok over low heat. Fry the balls in batches, till golden brown. Drain and set aside till cool.

Grind the balls in a mixer. Add the khoya and give the mixer another whirl.

Put 1 tbsp of ghee in a kadhai or wok over low heat. When hot, add the cardamoms and cinnamon. Mix in the ground wheat and khoya. Stir for 1 minute, remove from heat and set aside to cool.

Mix in the sugar and almonds.

To serve
Heat the dal.

Place the bati in a serving bowl, whole or crushed, and pour the dal over it. Garnish with coriander leaves and serve hot with the churma on the side.

Millet Stew

6 servings

- 1 cup pearl millet/bajra
- 2 medium onions, cut into wedges
- 2 medium potatoes, cut into large chunks
- 2 medium carrots, cut into large slices
- 1 cup sliced celery
- 200 gms mushrooms, chopped
- 2 bay leaves/tej patta
- ½ tsp dried basil
- ½ tsp dried thyme

Toast the millet in a dry frying pan over moderate heat for about 5 minutes, tossing continuously to prevent burning.

Place all ingredients in an ovenproof dish with 4 cups of water.

Cover the dish and cook in an oven preheated to 100°C for 8 hours.

Raise the temperature to 150°C and cook for another 4 hours.

Serve hot.

Chholar Dal (Spicy Yellow Lentils)

8 servings

2½ cups pigeon peas/tuvar
  dal/arhar dal
3 bay leaves/tej patta
3 whole dried red chillies
2 tbsp mustard oil
½ fresh coconut, very finely
  chopped
1½ tsp cumin seeds/jeera
½ tsp ginger paste
½ tsp red chilli powder
1 tsp freshly ground cumin
  powder/jeera
2 tsp salt
1 tsp chopped coriander
  leaves/hara dhania
3 tsp sugar
1 tbsp ghee
2 tsp garam masala powder

Wash the dal and drain. Pressure-cook the dal with the bay leaves, red chillies and 5 cups of water for 15-20 minutes after the cooker reaches full pressure.

Open the cooker when cool and leave it over high heat for 15-20 minutes.

Put the oil in a pan over low heat. When hot, fry the coconut till it starts to turn pink.

Add the cumin seeds and fry for a couple of minutes.

Mix in the ginger, chilli powder, cumin powder, salt and coriander leaves.

Sauté for 2-3 minutes.

Pour in the dal and stir well, till all the grains of the dal are mashed. Add a little water if necessary. Add the sugar.

Just before serving, stir in the ghee and garam masala powder.

Sambar

6 servings

Spice powder
½ tsp coconut oil
¼ tsp husked black gram/urad dal
2 tbsp coriander seeds/dhania
¼ tsp fenugreek seeds/methi
4 dried red chillies, split in half

Sambar
1 cup husked red lentils/ masoor dal
½ tsp turmeric powder/haldi
1 sprig + 1 sprig of curry leaves
A golf-ball-sized tamarind piece soaked in 1 cup of water
1 tsp red chilli powder
¼ tsp asafoetida powder/hing
¼ tsp grated jaggery/gud
1½ tsp salt
2 tbsp coconut oil
½ bitter gourd/karela, sliced lengthwise
1 aubergine/baingan, sliced lengthwise
1 drumstick/surjan ki phalli, cut into 2" sticks
4 okra/bhindi, sliced lengthwise

Tempering
2 tsp coconut oil
2 dried red chillies, split in half
1 tsp mustard seeds/rai/sarson

Garnish
1 tbsp chopped coriander leaves/hara dhania

Spice powder
Heat the oil in a small pan over moderate heat. Add the remaining spice paste ingredients. Toss for a few seconds and remove from heat. Cool and grind the contents of the pan into a fine powder. Set aside.

Sambar
Wash the dal and drain.

Bring 3 cups of water to a boil, add the dal and cook for about 15 minutes, till tender.

Add the turmeric powder and 1 sprig of curry leaves and set aside.

Extract the tamarind pulp and put it in a pan over moderate heat. Add 1 sprig of curry leaves, the chilli powder, asafoetida powder, jaggery and salt and bring to a boil. Pour in 2 tbsp of coconut oil.

Add the vegetables, except the okra, and cook till they are tender.

Pour in the dal, bring to a boil and add the okra and spice paste. Bring to a boil again and remove from heat.

Put the oil for tempering in a small pan over moderate heat. When hot, add the remaining tempering ingredients. When the mustard seeds splutter, pour the contents of the pan into the sambar.

Garnish with the coriander leaves and serve.

Pindi Chhole (Rawalpindi Chickpeas)

4 servings

1 cup chickpeas/kabuli chana
2 tbsp husked Bengal gram/
  chana dal
2 black cardamoms/badi
  elaichi
1" stick cinnamon/dalchini
2 tsp tea leaves tied in a
  muslin bag
¼ tsp sodium bicarbonate

Masala
2 tbsp oil
2 medium onions, finely
  chopped
1½ tsp pomegranate seed
  powder/anardana
1 large tomato, finely
  chopped
1" piece ginger, finely
  chopped
1 green chilli, finely chopped
½ tsp garam masala powder
1 tsp coriander powder/
  dhania
½ tsp red chilli powder
1 tsp chana masala
  (commercial)
1 tsp salt

Wash the chickpeas and gram and soak them together overnight in water or for 6-8 hours. Drain and rinse thoroughly.

Transfer the chickpeas and dal to a pressure cooker. Add the whole spices, tea leaves and sodium bicarbonate. Pour in enough water to cover contents of cooker. Pressure-cook for 20-25 minutes after the cooker reaches full pressure. Set aside till cool.

Put the oil for the masala in a pan over moderate heat. When hot, sauté the onions till translucent.

Sprinkle in the pomegranate seed powder. Stir-fry till the onions turn dark brown.

Add the tomato, ginger and green chilli. Stir-fry for 3-4 minutes.

Sprinkle in the garam masala, coriander and chilli powders. Stir-fry, mashing the tomatoes till they turn brownish and the oil floats to the surface.

Strain the chickpeas and gram, reserving the liquid. Remove and discard the tea bag.

Add the chickpeas and gram to the pan. Mix well and cook gently for 5-7 minutes.

Add the chana masala, salt and the reserved cooking liquid. Cook for 15-20 minutes over moderate heat till the liquid evaporates a little and the gravy is thick.

Serve hot.

MILLET STEW

Vagharia (Sweet and Sour Chickpeas)

4 servings

1 cup chickpeas/kabuli chana
6 black kokum, soaked in
 ¼ cup water
1 tbsp red chilli powder
¼ tsp turmeric powder/haldi
1 tbsp grated jaggery/gud
1 tbsp gram flour/besan
1½ tsp salt

Tempering
1½ tbsp oil
½ tsp mustard seeds/rai/
 sarson
A sprig of curry leaves
2-3 pinches of asafoetida
 powder/hing

Garnish
1 tbsp finely chopped
 coriander leaves / hara
 dhania

Wash the chickpeas and soak them overnight in water or for 6-8 hours. Drain and rinse thoroughly.

Pressure-cook the chickpeas with 1½ cups of water for 20 minutes after the cooker reaches full pressure. Set aside till cool.

Put the oil for tempering in a large pan over moderate heat. When hot, add the mustard seeds. When they splutter, add the remaining tempering ingredients. Stir in the kokum with its soaking liquid.

Sprinkle in the remaining spice powders and jaggery and stir-fry for a minute.

Add the chickpeas with its cooking liquid and bring to a boil.

Mix the gram flour with ¼ cup of water and pour it into the pan. Cook, stirring continuously, till the contents come to a boil again. Lower heat and simmer till the gravy is fairly thick.

Add salt, stir and garnish with coriander leaves. Serve hot with steamed rice or paratha.

Kala Chana Rasedar (Spicy Whole Bengal Gram)

4 servings

1¼ cups whole Bengal gram/
  kala chana
¼ tsp sodium bicarbonate
1 bay leaf/tej patta
2 black cardamoms/badi
  elaichi
1" stick cinnamon/dalchini
¾ tsp turmeric powder/haldi
1½ tsp salt
2 tsp coriander powder/
  dhania
¼ tsp red chilli powder
2 medium tomatoes, chopped
¼ tsp garam masala powder
¼ cup chopped coriander
  leaves/hara dhania

Tempering
2-3 tbsp oil
1 tsp cumin seeds/jeera
A large pinch of asafoetida
  powder/hing (optional)

Ground to a paste
2 medium onions, quartered
3 garlic cloves, roughly
  chopped
1" piece ginger, roughly
  chopped

Wash the gram and soak it overnight in water with the sodium bicarbonate or for 6-8 hours. Drain and rinse thoroughly.

Pressure-cook the gram with the bay leaf, whole spices, turmeric powder, salt and 1 litre of water for 20-30 minutes after the cooker reaches full pressure.

Open the cooker when cool and check that the gram is tender. Cook for 10 minutes longer if necessary. Set aside in the cooker.

Put the oil for tempering in a pan over moderate heat. When hot, add the cumin seeds and asafoetida powder (if used). When the cumin seeds splutter, add the ground onion paste and stir-fry till well browned.

Sprinkle in the coriander and chilli powders and stir for a few seconds.

Blend in the tomatoes and stir-fry till the oil floats to the surface.

Spoon the contents of the pan into the pressure cooker. Add more water if needed and pressure cook for 5 minutes.

Open the cooker when cool. Mix in the garam masala powder and half the coriander leaves.

Garnish with the remaining coriander leaves and serve hot.

Chana Dal aur Ghia (Bengal Gram with Bottle Gourd)

8 servings

500 gms husked Bengal
    gram/chana dal
2 tsp turmeric powder/haldi
2 tsp salt
1 bottle gourd/ghia/lauki
1 tbsp oil
2 bay leaves/tej patta
1 medium onion, chopped
1 tsp garam masala powder
1 tsp red chilli powder

Tempering
1 tbsp ghee
1 bay leaf/tej patta
2 cloves/lavang

Wash the gram and cook it with the turmeric powder, salt and enough water to cover for about 20 minutes, till tender. Set aside.

Peel the gourd, cut it into large chunks and set aside.

Heat the oil in a pan over moderate heat. Add the bay leaves and onion. Stir-fry till the onion is translucent.

Add the gourd and cook till tender.

Stir in the remaining spice powders. Gently mix in the dal.

Put the ghee for tempering in a small pan over low heat. When hot, add the bay leaf and cloves. Give it a stir and pour the contents of the pan into the gram and gourd.

Serve hot.

Gatte ka Saag (Steamed Gram Flour Dumplings in a Spicy Gravy)

4 servings

Gatte
1¼ cups gram flour/besan
½ cup sour yogurt/dahi
3 tbsp oil
¼ tsp red chilli powder
1 tsp turmeric powder/haldi

Tempering
¾ cup oil
3 tsp cumin seeds/jeera

Gravy
1½ cups sour yogurt/dahi
1¾ tsp red chilli powder
1 tbsp coriander powder/
   dhania
1½ tsp salt

Gatte
Sift the gram flour into a bowl and add the remaining gatte ingredients. Knead to prepare a soft dough.

Apply a little oil on your hands and roll the dough into 1"x 6" cylinders.

Bring plenty of water to a boil in a pan over high heat. Lower the heat and slide in the rolls. Cook for 5-7 minutes or till they become firm. Drain the rolls and set aside to cool for 15 minutes.

Cut the rolls into ¾" pieces.

Put the oil for tempering in a pan over moderate heat. When hot, add the cumin seeds. When they splutter, add the gatte and stir-fry for 1-2 minutes.

Gravy
Combine the yogurt in a bowl with the spice powders, mix well and add to the gatte. Stir and cook for 2-3 minutes.

Add the salt and 1 cup of water. Bring to a boil, lower the heat and simmer for 5-7 minutes, till the oil floats to the surface.

If the gravy is too thick, add a little more water.

Serve hot.

Masoor Dal (Red Lentils)

2-3 servings

1 cup husked red lentils/
   masoor dal
¼ tsp fenugreek seeds/methi
1 garlic clove, crushed
A sprig of curry leaves
1 small tomato, finely
   chopped
1 tsp red chilli powder
¼ tsp turmeric powder/haldi
¼ tsp coriander powder/
   dhania
¼ tsp garam masala powder
¼ tsp cumin powder/jeera
1½ tsp salt
½ lime, juice extracted
1 tbsp finely chopped
   coriander leaves/hara
   dhania
2 green chillies, slit

Tempering
2 tbsp ghee or oil
¼ tsp mustard seeds/rai/
   sarson
¼ tsp cumin seeds/jeera
2-3 pinches of asafoetida
   powder/hing

Wash the dal and soak it in water for about 30 minutes.

Bring 1 litre of water to a boil in a deep pan. Drain the dal and add it to the pan with the fenugreek seeds. Cover the pan and simmer over low heat for 1 hour, till the dal is mushy.

Put the ghee or oil for tempering in another pan over moderate heat. When hot, add the remaining tempering ingredients. When the mustard seeds splutter, stir in the garlic, curry leaves and tomato.

Sprinkle in the spice powders, salt and 2 tbsp of water. Stir and cook for a few seconds.

Add the cooked dal, stir and bring to a boil. Lower the heat, cover the pan and simmer for 2-3 minutes.

Remove from heat and stir in the lime juice, coriander leaves and green chillies.

Serve hot with steamed rice or cumin pulao (page 96).

Dal Makhani (Creamy Black Gram)

4 servings

1 cup whole black gram/
    sabut urad
2 tbsp husked Bengal gram/
    chana dal
2 tbsp kidney beans/rajma
1 tbsp + 3 tbsp ghee or oil
1½ tsp salt
2 dried red chillies
1" piece ginger, crushed
4 garlic cloves, crushed
    (optional)
4 medium tomatoes, puréed
2 tsp coriander powder/
dhania
½ tsp garam masala powder
1 tbsp dried fenugreek leaves/
    kasuri methi
1 tbsp tomato ketchup
2 tbsp butter
½ cup fresh cream, whisked

Wash both grams and the beans and soak them together in water for 6 hours or overnight. Drain and rinse well.

Pressure-cook the grams and beans with 6 cups of water, 1 tbsp of ghee or oil, salt, red chillies and half the ginger and garlic for 40 minutes after the cooker reaches full pressure.

Open the cooker after the pressure drops and mash the hot gram and beans lightly. Set aside.

Put 3 tbsp of ghee in a pan over moderate heat. When hot, add the tomatoes. Cook till thick and dry.

Add the remaining ginger and garlic and spice powders and stir-fry till the ghee or oil floats to the surface.

Mix in the fenugreek leaves and tomato ketchup. Stir and cook for 1-2 minutes.

Pour the contents of the pan into the cooker containing the boiled gram and beans.

Stir in the butter. Simmer over low heat for 20-25 minutes, stirring and mashing the gram and beans occasionally with a ladle against the sides of the cooker.

Add the cream. Mix well and simmer for 15-20 minutes, to get the right colour and smoothness.

Serve hot.

Khatta Dhokla (Steamed Black Gram Dumplings)

6-8 servings

1 cup husked red lentils/
masoor dal
¼ tsp fenugreek seeds/methi
1 garlic clove, crushed
A sprig of curry leaves
1 small tomato, finely
chopped
1 tsp red chilli powder
¼ tsp turmeric powder/haldi
¼ tsp coriander powder/
dhania
¼ tsp garam masala powder
¼ tsp cumin powder/jeera
1½ tsp salt
½ lime, juice extracted
1 tbsp finely chopped
coriander leaves/hara
dhania
2 green chillies, slit

Tempering
2 tbsp ghee or oil
¼ tsp mustard seeds/rai/
sarson
¼ tsp cumin seeds/jeera
2-3 pinches of asafoetida
powder/hing powder

Wash the dal and soak it in water for about 30 minutes.

Bring 1 litre of water to a boil in a deep pan. Drain the dal and add it to the pan with the fenugreek seeds. Cover the pan and simmer over low heat for 1 hour, till the dal is mushy.

Put the ghee or oil for tempering in another pan over moderate heat. When hot, add the remaining tempering ingredients. When the mustard seeds splutter, stir in the garlic, curry leaves and tomato.

Sprinkle in the spice powders, salt and 2 tbsp of water. Stir and cook for a few seconds.

Add the cooked dal, stir and bring to a boil. Lower the heat, cover the pan and simmer for 2-3 minutes.

Remove from heat and stir in the lime juice, coriander leaves and green chillies.

Serve hot with steamed rice or cumin pulao (page 96).

Bhaja Mung Dal (Roasted Mung Beans)

4 servings

1½ cups split mung beans/
chilke mung dal
1 tsp sugar
1½ tsp salt

Tempering
1 tbsp oil
2 tsp fennel seeds/saunf
3 cloves/lavang
3 green chillies, slit

Roast the dal on a tava or griddle, tossing continuously till golden brown.

Bring 2 cups of water to a boil in a pan over moderate heat, add the dal and cook for about 15 minutes, till tender.

Put the oil for tempering in a small pan over moderate heat. When hot, add the remaining tempering ingredients. Sauté just for a few seconds and pour the contents of the pan into the dal.

Add the sugar and salt, stir well and serve immediately.

Mung and Spinach Soup

4 servings

200 gms spinach/palak
1 tbsp husked mung beans/
mung dal
1 tbsp butter
1 tbsp super-refined wheat
flour/maida
½ cup milk
1½ tsp salt
½ tsp freshly ground black
pepper/kali miri

Pluck the spinach leaves and discard the stems. Wash the spinach leaves in several changes of water. Drain and set aside. Wash the dal and drain.

Pressure-cook the spinach and dal with 1½ cups of water for 10 minutes after the cooker reaches full pressure. Cool and blend the spinach and dal to a smooth purée.

Melt the butter in a pan over moderate heat. Add the flour and cook, stirring continuously till it sizzles.

Pour in the milk and stir vigorously to avoid lumps. Cook, stirring continuously, till it comes to a boil.

Add the puréed spinach and dal, salt and pepper and simmer for 4-5 minutes, stirring occasionally. Serve hot.

Naurangi Dal (Spicy Rice Beans)

2 servings

1 cup rice bean lentil/naurangi dal (see note)
¼ cup oil
1 medium onion, chopped
1" piece ginger, crushed
5 garlic cloves, chopped
1 tsp red chilli powder
½ tsp turmeric powder/haldi
1 tsp coriander powder/ dhania
1 tsp salt
1 medium tomato, chopped
1 tsp garam masala powder
2 tbsp chopped coriander leaves/hara dhania
2 green chillies, chopped

Note

Rice bean is a multicoloured bean; it has 9 different colours.

Wash the dal in several changes of water till the water runs clear. Soak in fresh water for about 1 hour. Drain the dal and set aside.

Put the oil in a pan over moderate heat. When hot, add the onion, ginger and garlic and stir-fry till the onion turns pale gold. Add 3-4 tbsp of water if the mixture sticks to the pan.

Add the chilli, turmeric and coriander powders, salt and about 5 tbsp of water to prevent the spices from burning. Stir-fry for about 5 minutes.

Mix in the tomato and continue to stir-fry for about 10 minutes till the tomatoes are reduced to a pulp and the oil floats to the surface. Add a little water, if necessary, to prevent the spices from sticking to the pan.

Add the drained dal and 2½ cups of water. Mix well, lower the heat, cover the pan and simmer for about 30 minutes, till the dal is tender and the water has evaporated.

Stir in the garam masala powder, coriander leaves and green chillies.

Serve hot with naan (page 126) or roti (page 123).

Rajma Madrah (Kidney Bean Stew)

6 servings

1 cup red kidney beans/rajma
½ tsp + 1 tsp salt
2 cups yogurt/dahi
1 tbsp gram flour/besan
1 tsp red chilli powder
½ tsp turmeric powder/haldi
½ tsp fenugreek seeds/methi,
   roasted and powdered
½ cup chopped cashew nuts
   and almonds
¼ cup seedless raisins/
   kishmish
¼ cup finely sliced dried
   coconut/kopra

Tempering
½ cup ghee
1 bay leaf/tej patta
1 tsp mixed whole garam
   masala

Wash the beans and soak them overnight in water. Drain and rinse thoroughly.

Place the beans in a pan with 2 cups of water and ½ tsp salt and cook till soft but not mushy.

Beat the yogurt and gram flour together in a bowl and set aside.

Put the ghee for tempering in a pan over moderate heat. When hot, add the bay leaf and whole spices. When they splutter, pour in the yogurt-gram flour mix and cook over low heat till it starts to turn brown.

Add the beans and 1 tsp salt and continue to cook for a few minutes.

Sprinkle in the spice powders and cook for a few minutes.

Add the nuts, raisins and coconut and serve hot.

Phaanu (Gravied Horse Gram Pancakes)

4 servings

Batter
1 cup horse gram/kulthi ka dal/gahath
3-4 green chillies
4-5 garlic cloves
½" piece ginger
1 tsp cumin seeds/jeera
Oil for frying

Gravy
½ cup oil
A pinch of asafoetida powder/hing
½ tsp coriander powder/dhania
¼ tsp turmeric powder/haldi
1½ tsp salt

Garnish
2 tbsp ghee
1 tbsp chopped coriander leaves/hara dhania

Wash the gram and soak it overnight in water. Wash and rub the gram under running water so that it is free of the seed coverings.

Drain the gram and mix it with the remaining batter ingredients, except the oil. Grind it into a thick batter, gradually adding about ½ cup of water.

Smear some oil on a tava or griddle and place it over moderate heat. When hot, pour a ladleful of the batter on the tava or griddle and spread it to make a ¼" thick pancake.

Drizzle oil around the sides and flip over when it is brown and cooked at the base. Fry till evenly brown on both sides.

Use half the batter to make more pancakes. Set the pancakes aside.

Mix the remaining batter with 3 cups of water to bring it to a pouring consistency.

Put the oil for the gravy in a pan over moderate heat. When hot, add the asafoetida powder. Give it a stir and mix in the reserved gram batter, remaining spice powders and salt.

Lower the heat, cover the pan and cook for about 10 minutes.

Add the pancakes to the gravy and continue simmering for another 10 minutes. The gravy should be of a pouring consistency. Add some water if it is too thick and heat till it boils.

Garnish with ghee and coriander leaves and serve hot with steamed rice.

Matki Fransbin Bhaji (Sprouted Brown Mung with French Beans)

8 servings

2 cups trimmed, chopped
  French beans
1½ cups sprouted brown
  mung beans/matki
A pinch of turmeric powder/
  haldi
1 tbsp goda masala
  (commercial) or garam
  masala powder
1 tsp red chilli powder
2-3 tbsp grated jaggery/gud
2 tsp salt
3 tbsp grated fresh coconut
  (optional)
3 tbsp chopped coriander
  leaves/hara dhania
  (optional)

Tempering
1 tsp oil
½ tsp mustard seeds/rai/
  sarson
A pinch of asafoetida powder/
  hing

Put the oil for tempering in a pan over moderate heat. When hot, add the mustard seeds. When they splutter, sprinkle in the asafoetida powder. Add the French beans, sprouts and turmeric powder.

Sprinkle in some water, cover the pan and steam-cook till the beans and sprouts are tender, but crunchy.

Add ¾ cup of hot water and the remaining ingredients, reserving a little coconut and coriander leaves (if used) for a garnish. Simmer very gently for 3-4 minutes.

Garnish with the reserved coconut and coriander leaves and serve hot.

Lobia-Palak (Black-Eyed Beans with Spinach)

4 servings

1 cup black-eyed beans/lobia
150 gms spinach/palak
1 tbsp oil
½ tsp cumin seeds/jeera
A pinch of asafoetida powder/
  hing
1" piece ginger, chopped
1 medium tomato, finely
  chopped
1 medium onion, finely
  chopped
2 green chillies, finely
  chopped
1 tsp lime juice
1 tsp red chilli powder
1 tsp coriander powder/
  dhania
½ tsp turmeric powder/haldi
½ tsp garam masala powder
1½ tsp salt

Garnish
½ cup finely chopped
  coriander leaves/hara
  dhania

Wash the beans and soak them in 3 cups of water for 4 hours.

Pluck the spinach leaves and discard the stalks. Wash the leaves in several changes of water and chop them.

Place the beans with the soaking liquid and the spinach in a deep pan over high heat. Bring to a boil and continue boiling for 12-15 minutes, till the beans are tender.

Heat the oil in a non-stick frying pan over moderate heat. Add the cumin seeds and asafoetida powder. Stir for 30 seconds and mix in the remaining ingredients, except the beans, spinach and garnish. Sprinkle in 2-3 tsp of water and cook for 5-7 minutes, stirring occasionally.

Transfer the contents of the pan to the pan containing the beans and spinach. Stir till well blended and heat through.

Garnish with coriander leaves and serve hot with roti, tortilla, bread or steamed rice.

Ras (Mixed Bean Soup)

8-10 servings

½ cup black soybeans/bhatt
¼ cup kidney beans/rajma
¼ cup black-eyed beans/lobia
¼ cup whole Bengal gram/
  kala chana
¼ cup chickpeas/kabuli
  chana
¼ cup whole black gram/
  sabut urad
½ cup horse gram/kulthi ka
  dal/gahath
1 tsp coriander powder/
  dhania
1 tsp cumin powder/jeera
½ tsp red chilli powder
½ tsp turmeric powder/haldi
½ tsp garam masala powder
3 tsp salt

Tempering
2 tbsp ghee
4-5 dried red chillies
A pinch of asafoetida powder/
  hing
A pinch of cumin seeds/jeera

Wash all the beans and gram and soak them overnight in water.

Drain and rinse the beans and gram and boil them in plenty of water till tender.

Mash well and strain the broth into a pan. Add some water to the residue and mash and strain the broth again into the same pan. Repeat till the water runs clear.

Put the broth over high heat and boil till it starts to thicken. Add the spice powders and salt.

When the broth has the consistency of a gravy, remove from heat.

Put the ghee for tempering in a small pan over moderate heat. When hot, add the remaining tempering ingredients. When they splutter, pour the contents of the pan into the ras.

Serve hot with steamed rice.

Bhatt ki Churdkani (Curried Black Soybeans)

4 servings

1 cup black soybeans/bhatt
2 tbsp oil
½ tsp cumin seeds/jeera
1 medium onion, chopped
1-2 tsp super-refined wheat
   flour/maida
1 tsp coriander powder/
   dhania
1 tsp cumin powder/jeera
½ tsp red chilli powder
¼ tsp turmeric powder/haldi
2 tsp salt

Wash the soybeans and soak them overnight in water. Drain and rinse the beans thoroughly. Set aside.

Put the oil in a kadhai or wok over moderate heat. When hot, add the cumin seeds and onion. Stir-fry till the onion turns brown.

Sprinkle in the flour and fry for a few minutes. Mix in the spice powders and salt and fry for a few seconds.

Add the beans and 4 cups of water and cook over high heat till it comes to a boil.

Lower the heat, cover the pan and simmer for 30-40 minutes, till the beans are tender and the curry is thick and dark, greenish black.

Serve hot with steamed rice.

Vegetable au Gratin

6 servings

½ cup wholewheat flour/
    gehun ka atta
2 tsp oil
1 medium onion, finely
    chopped
½" piece ginger, grated
1 green chilli, finely chopped
2 cups chopped mixed
    vegetables, boiled
½ tsp salt
¼ tsp freshly ground black
    pepper/kali miri
4 cups milk
1 tbsp grated cottage cheese/
    paneer

Sift the flour into a dry pan. Place it over low heat and toss till you get the aroma of roasted wheat. Do not let it brown. Remove the flour from the pan and set aside till cool.

Put the oil in the same pan and place it over moderate heat. When hot, sauté the onion till translucent.

Sprinkle in the flour and stir and cook over low heat for 2-3 minutes.

Stir in the ginger and green chilli. Add the vegetables, salt and pepper.

Pour in the milk and stir vigorously till the sauce is smooth and without lumps. Continue stirring till the sauce comes to a boil. Lower heat and simmer till it is thick, stirring continuously.

Taste and add more salt or pepper if required.

Transfer the contents of the pan to a shallow ovenproof dish. Sprinkle cheese on top and allow it to cool completely.

Bake in an oven preheated to 200°C for about 15 minutes till golden brown on top.

Serve hot.

Hyderabadi Baingan (Hyderabadi Aubergines)

6 servings

Aubergines
500 gms small aubergines/
   baingan
2 tsp salt
3 tbsp oil
1½ tsp cumin seeds/jeera
½ tsp fenugreek seeds/methi
10-12 curry leaves
½ tsp turmeric powder/haldi
½ tsp red chilli powder

Spice paste
¼ cup peanuts
¼ cup chopped onion
1 tsp sesame seeds/til
1 tsp cumin seeds/jeera
2 tsp coriander seeds/dhania

Gravy
2 tbsp oil
1 tbsp tamarind pulp
Green chillies to taste
1 tbsp chopped coriander
   leaves/hara dhania
1½ tsp salt

Aubergines
Cut the aubergines at the base to make a cross coming halfway up. Leave the stems intact and soak them in salted water.

Heat 3 tbsp of oil in a pan and sprinkle in the whole spices, curry leaves and spice powders.

Drain the aubergines and add them to the pan. Fry for about 10 minutes. Remove the pan from heat and set aside.

Spice paste
Roast the peanuts and the onion together in a dry frying pan over moderate heat till fragrant. Cool and grind to a paste with the remaining spice paste ingredients, adding a little water if required.

Gravy
Put the oil in a pan over moderate heat. When hot, fry the ground paste for about 3 minutes. Mix in the remaining gravy ingredients with ½ cup of water. Simmer for a few minutes.

Add the aubergines to the gravy and simmer for about 10 minutes.

Serve hot.

Potatoes with Black Pepper

4 servings

4 medium potatoes
1 tbsp oil
3 tsp, black pepper powder/
  kali miri
1 tsp salt
3 tsp chopped coriander
  leaves/hara dhania

Scrub the potatoes and boil them in their jackets. When cool enough to handle, peel and cut into ¾" cubes.

Put the oil in a pan over moderate heat. When hot, add the potatoes, pepper and salt. Fry tossing frequently, till the potatoes have a slight crust on them.

Add the coriander leaves, stir briefly and serve.

New Potatoes with Green Peas and Coriander

4 servings

10 small new potatoes
½ cup shelled green peas
½ tsp turmeric powder/haldi
1½ tsp minced ginger
2 small green chillies,
  chopped
¼ cup chopped coriander
  leaves/hara dhania
1 tsp salt
1 tsp red chilli powder
1 tsp garam masala powder
1 tbsp coriander seeds/
  dhania
2 tsp lime juice

Tempering
1 tbsp ghee
1 tsp cumin seeds/jeera

Scrub the potatoes thoroughly, leave unpeeled and dice them.

Put the ghee for tempering in a pan over low heat. When hot, add the cumin seeds and toss for about a minute.

Add the potatoes and fry for about 5 minutes, tossing frequently. Mix in the green peas and fry, stirring continuously for about 2 minutes.

Add the turmeric powder, ginger and green chillies. Cook stirring occasionally, for about 3 minutes.

Add the remaining ingredients and sprinkle in about 6 tbsp of water.

Lower the heat, cover the pan and simmer for about 15 minutes. Stir occasionally and add more water if necessary.

Raise heat to moderate and cook uncovered till the vegetables are tender and all the water evaporates. Serve hot.

Batata Bhaji (Stir-Fried Potatoes)

4 servings

6-7 medium potatoes
1 medium onion, finely sliced
¼ tsp turmeric powder/haldi
1½ tsp salt
½ cup grated fresh coconut

Tempering
3 tbsp oil
½ tsp mustard seeds/rai/
   sarson
4-5 curry leaves
2 tbsp husked black gram/
   urad dal
2 dried red chillies, broken
   into 2-3 pieces

Garnish
¼ cup chopped coriander
   leaves/hara dhania

Parboil the potatoes in their jackets. Peel and cut into 1" cubes.

Put the oil for tempering in a kadhai or wok over moderate heat. When hot, add the mustard seeds. When they splutter, add the curry leaves and gram. Sauté till the gram turns light brown.

Add the red chillies and when they change colour add the onion. Fry till the onion turns translucent.

Sprinkle in the turmeric powder. Add the potatoes and salt and mix gently. Cook covered for about 5 minutes, till the potatoes are tender. Mix in the coconut and remove from heat.

Garnish with coriander leaves and serve hot.

Potato Sticks with Mustard Seeds

6 servings

8 medium potatoes
6 tbsp olive oil
2 garlic cloves, finely chopped
1 tbsp finely chopped ginger
1 tbsp yellow mustard seeds/
   rai/sarson
½ tsp salt
¼ tsp black pepper powder/
   kali miri

Garnish
½ cup chopped coriander
   leaves/hara dhania

Peel the potatoes and cut them crosswise into ¼" thick sticks. Boil till tender.

Drain and transfer carefully to a platter, using a wide spatula to avoid breaking the sticks.

Put the oil in a frying pan over moderate-low heat. When hot, add the garlic and ginger and stir for about 1 minute, till they begin to sizzle.

Add the mustard seeds, salt and pepper and cook, stirring for 1-2 minutes, till the garlic is pale golden.

Spoon the contents of the pan over the potatoes, garnish with coriander leaves and serve hot.

Mashed Potatoes with Chilli and Ginger

4 servings

4 large potatoes, cut into
   1" cubes
1½ cups buttermilk/chaas or
   yogurt/dahi
1 green chilli, chopped
1 tsp salt
½ tsp black pepper powder/
   kali miri
¼ cup ghee
1" piece ginger, minced

Garnish
2 tbsp chopped coriander
   leaves/hara dhania

Cook the potatoes in a large pan of boiling water for about 15 minutes, till tender. Drain the potatoes and return them to the pan. Mash them coarsely with a potato masher.

Add the buttermilk or yogurt and green chilli and mash till smooth. Season with salt and pepper.

Heat the ghee and ginger in a small pan. Cook over low heat, stirring occasionally for about 3 minutes.

Stir the contents of the pan into the potatoes.

Garnish with coriander leaves and serve hot.

Fenugreek Potatoes

8 servings

4 cups cubed potatoes
¼ tsp asafoetida powder/hing
1 tsp red chilli powder
1 tbsp coriander powder/
   dhania
¼ tsp turmeric powder/haldi
½ tsp fenugreek seeds/methi
2 tsp salt
½ cup chopped coriander
   leaves/hara dhania

Tempering
2 tsp oil
1 tsp mustard seeds/rai/
   sarson

Put the oil for tempering in a kadhai or wok over moderate heat. When hot, add the mustard seeds. When they splutter, add the potatoes and asafoetida powder. Stir for 1 minute.

Sprinkle in the remaining spice powders, fenugreek seeds and salt. Stir till the potatoes are well coated with spices. Cook stirring occasionally, till the potatoes are crisp and tender.

Mix in the coriander leaves and serve hot.

Kashmiri Dum Alu (Kashmiri Slow-Cooked Potatoes)

5 servings

500 gms baby potatoes
Mustard oil for deep-frying
1½ cup yogurt/dahi
½ tbsp gram flour/besan
1½ tsp red chilli powder
1½ tsp salt
½ tsp ginger powder/saunth
¾ tsp fennel powder/saunf

Ground to a fine powder
4 green cardamoms/chhoti
  elaichi
5 cloves/lavang
2 x 1" sticks cinnamon/
  dalchini

Parboil the potatoes and peel them while still warm. Pierce each potato 2-3 times with a thin wooden toothpick.

Put the oil in a kadhai or wok over moderate heat. When hot, fry the potatoes till they rise to the surface and are golden brown. Drain the potatoes and place on kitchen paper to absorb excess oil.

Mix the yogurt, gram flour, chilli powder and salt with 1 cup of water in a bowl. Whisk well, till smooth and free of lumps.

Put 4 tbsp of the oil used to fry the potatoes in another pan over moderate heat. Remove from heat, allow it to cool slightly and pour it into the yogurt, stirring continuously.

Transfer the yogurt to the same pan and bring to a boil, stirring continuously.

Add the potatoes, ginger powder, fennel powder and ground spices. Cook over moderate heat for 5-10 minutes, till the gravy thickens.

Serve hot.

Methi Bhaji (Sautéed Fresh Fenugreek)

4 servings

250 gms fenugreek leaves/
  methi
1 large tomato, chopped
½ tsp red chilli powder
¼ tsp coriander powder/
  dhania
½ tsp turmeric powder/haldi
2 tsp salt

Tempering
1 tbsp oil
¼ tsp mustard seeds/rai/
  sarson
¼ tsp cumin seeds/jeera
¼ tsp asafoetida powder/hing

Pluck the fenugreek leaves and discard the stems. Wash the leaves in several changes of water, drain and chop them coarsely.

Bring 1 litre of water to a boil and add the fenugreek leaves. Lower the heat and simmer for 2-3 minutes.

Drain the leaves through a colander and rinse under running water. Press out excess water and set aside.

Put the oil for tempering in a pan over moderate heat. When hot, add the mustard and cumin seeds and asafoetida powder. When the mustard seeds splutter, mix in the tomato, spice powders and salt.

Simmer over low heat till the oil floats to the surface.

Pour in 1 tbsp of water, bring to a boil and stir in the fenugreek leaves.

Mix well and cook over low heat till the oil floats to the surface.

Serve hot with thin roti or phulka (page 123).

Sarson ka Saag (Sautéed Mustard Greens)

4 servings

150 gms mustard greens/
  sarson
150 gms spinach/palak
1 tbsp oil
3 green chillies
½ tsp grated ginger
½ tsp grated garlic
1 tsp salt
2 tbsp ghee
1 medium onion, grated
½ tsp garam masala powder
1 tbsp maize flour/makki ka
  atta
½ lime, juice extracted

Pluck the leaves of the mustard greens and spinach and discard the stems. Wash the leaves in several changes of water, drain and chop them.

Put the oil in a pressure cooker over moderate heat. When hot, stir in the greens and green chillies. Mix in the ginger and garlic. Add a few pinches of salt and 1 cup of water and mix well. Pressure-cook for 30 minutes after the cooker reaches full pressure.

Open the cooker when cool and mash the contents well. Set aside.

Put the ghee in a pan over moderate heat. When hot, sauté the onion, till brown.

Stir in the mashed greens, garam masala powder, maize flour, lime juice and remaining salt. Cook till the oil floats to the surface.

Serve hot with makki ki roti (page 135) or paratha (page 124).

Bendakaya Pulusu (Okra in Tamarind Gravy)

4 servings

250 gms okra/bhindi
2 medium onions, chopped
A sprig of curry leaves
¼ tsp asafoetida powder/hing
1½ tsp turmeric powder/haldi
½ tsp red chilli powder
2 tsp sambar masala
  (commercial)
1½ tsp salt
3 green chillies, chopped
A lemon-sized ball of
  tamarind, soaked in ¼ cup
  warm water

Tempering
5 tbsp oil
½ tsp mustard seeds/rai/
  sarson

Wash the okra and dry on a kitchen towel immediately. Top and tail the okra and cut into 1" pieces.

Put the oil for tempering in a frying pan over moderate heat. When hot, add the mustard seeds. When they splutter, add the onions. Sauté till the onions turn translucent.

Add the curry leaves, spice powders, salt and green chillies.

Mix in the okra and sauté over low heat for about 5 minutes.

Extract the tamarind pulp and add it to the pan with about ½ cup of water to thin the gravy. Boil till the okra are cooked.

Simmer over low heat for 10 minutes longer and serve hot.

Cabbage with Fennel and Onions

6 servings

2 medium onions, sliced
500 gms cabbage, shredded
1 tbsp lime juice
1¾ tsp salt
1 tsp garam masala powder
4 cups cooked basmati rice,
   kept warm

Tempering
1 tsp oil
5 fenugreek seeds/methi
½ tsp cumin seeds/jeera
¼ tsp mustard seeds/rai/
   sarson
½ tsp fennel seeds/saunf

Ground to a paste
1 large, ripe tomato
2 garlic cloves
1½" piece ginger
½ tsp turmeric powder/haldi
1 green chilli

Put the oil for tempering in a pan over moderate heat. When hot, add the whole spices.

When they splutter and change colour, add the onions.

Sauté for about 3 minutes, till light brown.

Add the cabbage and stir-fry for a few minutes to release the juices.

Stir in the tomato-spice paste. Cover the pan and cook over low heat till the cabbage is tender.

Add the lime juice and salt and cook for about 5 minutes.

Sprinkle in the garam masala powder.

Place the rice in a serving dish and spoon the contents of the pan over it.

Punjabi Kadhi (Yogurt Curry with Gram Flour Dumplings)

6 servings

Pakoda
1 cup gram flour/besan
¼ cup chopped onion
¼ cup chopped potato
1 tsp ajwain
1 tsp red chilli powder
1 tsp chopped ginger
½ tsp baking powder
½ tsp salt
Oil for deep-frying

Kadhi
1 cup yogurt/dahi
¼ cup gram flour/besan
1 tsp turmeric powder/haldi
1 tsp salt
1 tsp red chilli powder

Tempering
2 tbsp oil
1 tsp fenugreek seeds/methi
2 whole dried red chillies
A pinch of asafoetida powder/
   hing

Pakoda
Sift the gram flour into a bowl. Add the remaining pakoda ingredients, except the oil, and mix well.

Gradually add about ½ cup of water and mix to prepare a smooth batter.

Put the oil in a kadhai or wok over moderate heat. When hot, drop spoonfuls of batter into the oil and fry the pakoda in batches, till golden brown.

Drain and place on kitchen paper to absorb excess oil.

Kadhi
Beat the yogurt in a bowl till smooth. Sift in the gram flour, blending it in well to avoid lumps.

Mix in the turmeric powder, salt and 3 cups of water.

Put the oil for tempering in a kadhai or wok over moderate heat. When hot, add the remaining tempering ingredients and stir-fry for 30 seconds.

Pour in the yogurt-gram flour mix. Bring to a boil, stirring continuously. Lower the heat and simmer for about 15 minutes, stirring occasionally.

To serve
Just before serving add the chilli powder and fried pakoda to the kadhi and simmer for about 5 minutes.

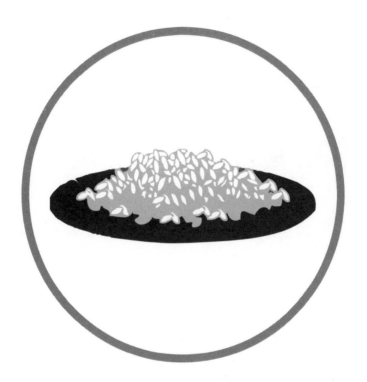

Rice Dishes for Lunch and Dinner

Kannadiga Khichdi

2 servings

1 cup rice
½ cup husked mung beans/
  mung dal
2 tsp salt

Tempering
1 tbsp ghee
1 tsp cumin seeds/jeera
1 tsp asafoetida powder/hing
1 tsp turmeric powder/haldi

Wash the rice and the dal and soak them together in water for 30 minutes. Drain and set aside.

Put the ghee in a pan over moderate heat. When hot, add the cumin seeds and spice powders. When the cumin seeds splutter, add the drained rice and dal.

Lower heat and stir gently for about 5 minutes. Add 3 cups of water and the salt and cook for about 10 minutes, till the water is absorbed and the rice and dal are tender and fluffy.

Serve hot.

Bihari Pulao

4 servings

2 cups basmati rice
½ cup shelled green peas
1 tsp garam masala powder
½ tsp salt

Tempering
2 tsp ghee
2 bay leaves/tej patta
1" stick cinnamon/dalchini
3 green cardamoms/chhoti
  elaichi

Wash the rice and soak it in water for about 30 minutes.

Put the ghee for tempering in a pan over moderate heat. When hot, add the remaining tempering ingredients. Give it a stir.

Drain the rice and mix it into the pan with the green peas and garam masala powder. Stir-fry for about 5 minutes.

Pour in 4 cups of water and mix in the salt. Cover the pan and cook for about 10 minutes, till the rice and green peas are tender. Serve hot.

Maharashtrian Pulao

4 servings

2 cups rice
2 cups chopped vegetables
    (potatoes, green peas,
    cauliflower, cabbage)
3½ tsp salt
2½ tbsp oil
2 medium onions, sliced
10 almonds or cashew nuts
2 tbsp seedless raisins/
    kishmish

Tempering
1½ tbsp oil
4 cloves/lavang
1" stick cinnamon/dalchini

Ground to a paste
10 green chillies, chopped
½ cup chopped coriander
    leaves/hara dhania
1 cup grated fresh coconut

Wash the rice. Drain and set aside.

Put the oil for tempering in a pan over moderate heat. When hot, toss in the cloves and cinnamon. Give it a stir.

Add the rice and stir gently for 1-2 minutes. Mix in the vegetables.

Pour in 4 cups of hot water and sprinkle in the salt. Stir and cook over low heat for 20 minutes, till the rice and vegetables are tender. (You can also cook it in a pressure-cooker for 3 minutes after the cooker reaches full pressure.)

Stir in the ground paste and cook over low heat for a few minutes.

Heat 2½ tbsp of oil in a small pan and fry the onions, nuts and raisins till the onions are brown.

Stir the contents of the pan into the pulao just before serving.

Kannadiga Tomato Pulao
2 servings

1 cup rice
½ fresh coconut, grated
4-5 medium tomatoes
2 medium onions, sliced
5-6 green chillies, slit
1½ tsp salt
2 tsp ghee

Tempering
3 tbsp ghee
2 green cardamoms /
   chhoti elaichi
1" stick cinnamon/dalchini
3-4 cloves/lavang

Wash the rice. Drain and set aside.

Grind the coconut with 1 cup of water in a mixer and press out the milk into a bowl, through a strainer lined with muslin. Set aside.

Place the tomatoes in boiling water till the skin is wrinkled. Drain and set aside till cool. Peel the tomatoes, cut into quarters and remove and discard the seeds. Purée the tomato flesh to make 1½ cups of juice.

Mix the coconut milk with the tomato juice and set aside.

Put the ghee for tempering in a pan over moderate heat. When hot, toss in the remaining tempering ingredients and give it a stir.

Add the onions and green chillies and sauté for 3-5 minutes.

Mix in the rice and sauté for 5 minutes.

Add the tomato-coconut milk mix and salt and simmer for about 10 minutes, till the rice is tender and fluffy.

Stir in the ghee, cover the pan and place in an oven preheated to 150°C-180°C for 10 minutes. This loosens the rice.

Serve with onion pachadi (page 140).

Kannadiga Fenugreek Pulao

2 servings

1 cup rice
250 gms fenugreek leaves/
methi
4 tbsp oil
9-10 garlic cloves, chopped
1 tsp red chilli powder
1 tsp turmeric powder/haldi
1 tsp salt

Ground to a paste
1 cup grated fresh coconut
2-3 x 1" sticks cinnamon/
dalchini
2 tsp black cumin seeds/
kala jeera
1½" piece ginger

Wash the rice, drain and set aside.

Pluck the fenugreek leaves and discard the stems. Wash the leaves in several changes of water, drain and chop them.

Put the oil in a pan over moderate heat. When hot, add the garlic, fenugreek leaves, chilli powder, turmeric powder and salt in that order.

Give it a stir and blend in the spice paste. Pour in 2 cups of water and bring to a boil.

Add the rice and cook it over low heat for about 10 minutes, till the water is absorbed and the rice is tender and fluffy.

Serve hot.

Cumin Pulao

4 servings

2½ cups long-grained rice
2 tbsp ghee
1 tsp cumin seeds/jeera
½ tsp salt

Wash the rice, drain and set aside.

Put the ghee in a heavy-based pan over moderate heat. When hot, add the cumin seeds. When they sputter add the rice and stir-fry gently for about 3 minutes till the rice turns translucent.

Add the salt and 3 cups of hot water. Stir and bring to a boil.

Cover the pan partially and simmer over low heat till the rice is tender and fluffy.

Serve hot.

Maharashtrian Cauliflower Rice

4-5 servings

3 cups basmati rice
1 fresh coconut, grated
2 large onions, sliced
500 gms cauliflower, cut into florets
½ cup chopped coriander leaves/hara dhania
2 tsp salt

Spice powder
5 cloves/lavang
1 tbsp coriander seeds/dhania
½ tsp black cumin seeds/kala jeera
1" stick cinnamon/dalchini
3-4 dried red chillies

Tempering
4 tbsp oil
4 cloves/lavang
4 green cardamoms/chhoti elaichi
1 tsp black cumin seeds/kala jeera

Wash the rice. Drain and set aside.

Grind the coconut with 6 cups of water in a mixer and press the milk into a bowl, through a strainer lined with muslin. Set aside.

Lightly roast the spice powder ingredients on a dry tava or griddle over moderate heat. Cool and grind to a fine powder. Set aside.

Put the oil for tempering in a pan over moderate heat. When hot, add the remaining tempering ingredients. When the cloves turn brown and the cumin seeds splutter, add the onions. Fry till light brown.

Add the rice and stir till it turns translucent. Gently mix in the cauliflower.

Pour in the coconut milk, spice powder, coriander leaves and salt.

Stir gently and simmer over low heat for about 10 minutes, till the rice is tender and fluffy.

Serve hot.

Note

If the rice is cooked in a pressure cooker only 5 cups of coconut milk are required.

Vangi Bhath (Aubergine Rice)

2 servings

1 cup rice
250 gms aubergines/baingan,
    cut lengthwise in 1" slices
A lemon-sized ball of
    tamarind soaked in
    ¼ cup water
½ tbsp salt
1 tsp + 1 tsp garam masala
    powder
¼ cup ghee or oil
3 large onions, chopped
    (optional)
¼ fresh coconut, grated
¼ cup chopped coriander
    leaves

Tempering
1 tbsp ghee or oil
4 cloves/lavang
2 x 1" sticks cinnamon/
    dalchini

Wash the rice. Drain and set aside.

Put the ghee or oil for the tempering in a pan over moderate heat. When hot, toss in the remaining tempering ingredients and give it a quick stir.

Add the rice and stir till it becomes translucent.

Add the aubergines and mix gently.

Extract the tamarind pulp and add it to the pan with the salt and 1 tsp garam masala powder. Stir well and add 2 cups of hot water.

Cook over low heat for about 5 minutes or in a pressure cooker till the cooker reaches full pressure. Remove from heat and set aside.

Pour the ghee or oil into a large pan over moderate heat.

Add the onions (if used) and fry till light brown.

Gently mix in the cooked rice. (If you are not using the onions, add the ghee to the rice.)

Sprinkle in 1 tsp of garam masala powder and stir lightly.

Cover the pan and cook for a few minutes over low heat, till the rice is tender and fluffy.

Mix in the coconut and coriander leaves and serve hot.

Puliyam Sadam (Tamarind Rice)

4 servings

2 cups rice

Puli kachal
A lime-sized ball of tamarind
   soaked in 2 cups of hot
   water
½ cup oil
¼ cup peanuts
1 tsp mustard seeds/rai/
   sarson
¼ tsp asafoetida powder/hing
   powder
¼ tsp turmeric powder/haldi
¾ tsp fenugreek seeds/methi,
   roasted and ground
½ tsp red chilli powder
1 tbsp coriander powder/
   dhania
1¼ tsp salt
A few sprigs of curry leaves
1 tbsp grated jaggery/gud

Puli Kachal
Extract the tamarind pulp and set aside.

Put 2 tbsp of oil in a frying pan over moderate heat. When hot, add the peanuts and toss for a few minutes.

Stir in the tamarind pulp and leave it over low heat.

Put the remaining oil in a small pan over moderate heat. When hot, add the mustard seeds and asafoetida powder. When the mustard seeds splutter, pour the contents of the pan into the pan containing the tamarind.

Add the remaining spice powders, salt and curry leaves. Mix well. Cook over moderate heat for 5-6 minutes, stirring occasionally, till the oil floats to the surface.

Mix in the jaggery and remove from heat.

Puliyam Sadam
Wash the rice and soak it in water for about 15 minutes.

Note

The puli kachal can be cooled and stored in a bottle for 20 days in the refrigerator.

Drain the rice and cook it over low heat with 4 cups of water for about 7 minutes, till the water is absorbed and the rice is tender and fluffy.

Mix the puli kachal into the rice and serve.

Yogurt Rice

2 servings

½ cup rice
2½ cups yogurt/dahi
4 green chillies, chopped
½" piece ginger, minced
1 tsp salt
A few coriander leaves/hara
   dhania, chopped

Tempering
2 tsp ghee
1 tsp husked Bengal gram/
   chana dal
1 tsp husked black gram/
   urad dal
½ tsp mustard seeds/rai/
   sarson
A sprig of curry leaves

Wash the rice and cook it in 1 cup of water for about 10 minutes, till the water is absorbed and the rice is fluffy and tender.

Whisk the yogurt till smooth and add the green chillies, ginger and salt. Mix in the rice.

Put the ghee for tempering over moderate heat. When hot, add the remaining tempering ingredients. When the mustard seeds splutter, mix the contents of the pan into the rice and yogurt, along with the coriander leaves.

Serve chilled or at room temperature.

Lemon Rice

4 servings

- 2 cups rice
- 4 tbsp chopped coriander leaves/hara dhania
- 3 green chillies, sliced
- ½ tsp turmeric powder/haldi
- 8-10 curry leaves
- 10-15 cashew nuts, chopped
- 2 large lemons or limes, juice extracted
- 2½ tsp salt

Tempering
- 1 tbsp ghee
- 1 tsp mustard seeds/rai/ sarson
- 1 tsp husked black gram/ urad dal
- 1 tsp husked Bengal gram/ chana dal

Wash the rice and cook it in 4 cups of water for about 10 minutes, till the water is absorbed and the rice is fluffy and tender. Set aside.

Put the ghee for tempering in a heavy-based pan over moderate heat. When hot, add the remaining tempering ingredients. When the mustard seeds splutter, add the coriander leaves (reserving a little for the garnish), green chillies, turmeric powder, curry leaves and cashew nuts.

Give it a stir and gently mix it into the cooked rice. Stir in the lemon or lime juice and salt.

Serve garnished with the reserved coriander leaves.

Bisi Bele Bhath (Spicy Rice and Lentils with Mixed Vegetables)

8 servings

4 cups rice
2 cups pigeon peas/tuvar dal/arhar dal
250 gms yellow pumpkin/kaddu,
    cut into 1" cubes
10 French beans, trimmed and chopped
4 medium onions, cut into 1" cubes
3 medium carrots, cut into 1" pieces
2 small cucumbers, cut into 1" pieces
2 sprigs of curry leaves
1 cup ghee or butter
1 cup peanuts, roasted
1 tbsp grated fresh coconut
4 tbsp chopped coriander leaves/
    hara dhania

Tempering
2 tbsp oil
1 tbsp husked Bengal gram/chana dal
1 tbsp husked black gram/urad dal
½ tsp mustard seeds/rai/sarson
¼ tsp cumin seeds/jeera
A pinch of asafoetida powder/hing

Roasted and ground to a fine powder
4 tbsp coriander seeds/dhania
2 tsp cumin seeds/jeera
2 tsp black cumin seeds/kala jeera
2 x 1" sticks cinnamon/dalchini
½ nutmeg/jaiphal
4 cloves/lavang
2 green cardamoms/chhoti elaichi
½ tsp black peppercorns/kali miri

Ground to a fine paste
½ fresh coconut, grated
20 dried red chillies
2 lemon-sized balls of tamarind,
    without seeds and strings
6 tsp salt

Wash the rice and soak it in water for 4 hours. Drain and set aside.

Wash the dal and pressure-cook it with 6 cups of water for 7 minutes after the cooker reaches full pressure. Set aside.

Put the oil for tempering in a pan over moderate heat. When hot, add the remaining tempering ingredients. When the mustard seeds splutter, add the vegetables, curry leaves and ½ cup of water and cook for about 5 minutes.

Pour in 8 cups of water and bring to a boil.

Mix the spice powder with the coconut paste and add it to the pan with the rice and dal.

Mix gently, cover the pan and simmer over low heat till the rice is half cooked, stirring occasionally.

Add the ghee or butter and cook till the rice, dal and vegetables are tender.

Stir in the peanuts, coconut and coriander leaves and serve hot.

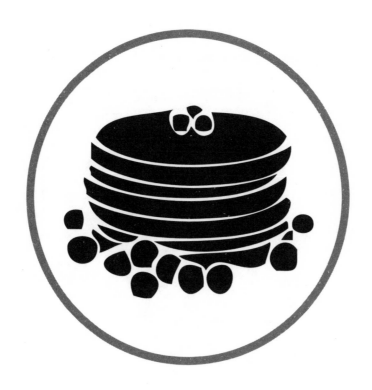

Snacks

Chira Bhaja (Fried Beaten Rice)

8 servings

Oil for deep-frying
4 cups beaten rice/poha
¼ cup peanuts
¼ cup potato juliennes
1 tbsp salt
1 tsp black peppercorns/
  kali miri, crushed

Heat the oil in a kadhai or wok and fry the beaten rice in batches over low heat. Drain and place on kitchen paper to absorb excess oil.

Fry the peanuts followed by the potatoes. Drain each and place on kitchen paper.

Combine the fried ingredients in a large mixing bowl. Add the salt and pepper, and mix gently till well blended.

Serve hot or at room temperature.

Badil (Mixed Lentil Cakes)

8-10 servings

1 cup horse gram/kulthi ka
   dal/gahath
2/3 cup husked Bengal gram/
   chana dal
2/3 cup pigeon peas/tuvar
   dal/arhar dal
2/3 cup husked mung beans/
   mung dal
3 tsp salt
½ cup oil or ghee for shallow-
   frying

Tempering
1 tsp oil
A pinch of asafoetida powder/
   hing
1 tsp ajwain

Ground to a paste
10 garlic cloves
1" piece ginger
3-4 green chillies
1 tsp cumin seeds/jeera
4 black peppercorns/kali miri
1" stick cinnamon/dalchini
4 cloves/lavang
½ tsp coriander powder/
   dhania
½ tsp turmeric powder/haldi
½ tsp red chilli powder
1-2 tbsp water

Garnish
2 tbsp chopped coriander
   leaves
2 tbsp grated fresh coconut

Wash the gram and dals together, drain them and set aside.

Put the oil for tempering in a large frying pan over moderate heat. When hot, add the remaining tempering ingredients.

Give it a stir and mix in the spice paste. Stir-fry for about 2 minutes.

Pour in 2 cups of water and the salt. Bring it to a boil and add the gram and dals. Cover the pan and cook for about 10 minutes, adding more water if required, till gram and dals are tender.

Crush and grind the cooked gram and dals with a ladle, till they do not stick to it.

Spoon the cooked batter into a lightly greased thali (a flat metal plate with a low rim). Spread the batter uniformly, and allow it to cool and solidify.

Cut into small cakes or badil.

Heat the oil or ghee in a frying pan and shallow-fry the badil over moderate heat, in batches, till brown on both sides. Drain and place on kitchen paper to absorb excess oil.

Garnish with coriander leaves and coconut and serve with date and tamarind chutney (page 143).

Finger Millet Crêpes

2 servings

1 cup finger millet flour/ragi/
   nachni ka atta
2 tbsp red chilli powder
¾ tsp salt
Butter for frying
1 medium capsicum/Shimla
   mirch, chopped
1 medium tomato, chopped
1 medium onion, chopped

Sift the flour into a bowl. Pour in ½ cup of water and mix to make a batter. Add the chilli powder and salt and mix well.

Put a non-stick tava or griddle over moderate heat and brush it lightly with butter.

Grasp the tava or griddle in one hand and pour ¼ cup of batter on to the pan while rotating it, so that a thin layer of batter covers the surface.

Return the pan to moderate heat. Cook for 2-3 minutes or till the top dries and the base is just light brown.

Sprinkle a little of the chopped vegetables on the top and cover the pan to let the vegetables steam-cook.

Remove the crêpe from the pan and keep warm.

Cook the remaining crêpes in the same way.

Serve warm with any filling of your choice.

Variation: Buckwheat flour can be used in place of the finger millet flour.

Missal Pav (Spicy Green and Brown Mung Sprouts)

4 servings

1 cup green mung bean
  sprouts
1 cup brown mung bean
  sprouts/matki
1 medium onion, finely
  chopped
2 green chillies, slit
1 tsp garlic paste
1 tsp ginger paste
½ tsp turmeric powder/haldi
1½ tsp red chilli powder
½ tsp coriander powder/
  dhania
½ tsp cumin powder/jeera
2 tsp salt
1 tsp garam masala powder
1 tbsp finely chopped
  coriander leaves/hara
  dhania

Tempering
2 tbsp oil
½ tsp mustard seeds/rai/
  sarson
A pinch of asafoetida powder/
  hing
A few curry leaves

To serve
½ cup gram flour strings/shev
1 medium onion, finely
  chopped
1 tbsp finely chopped
  coriander leaves/
  hara dhania
Lime juice as required
Lime slices as required
8 bread rolls/pav

Mix the sprouts in a colander and wash under running water for a minute. Drain and set aside.

Put the oil for tempering in a pan over moderate heat. When hot, add the mustard seeds, asafoetida powder and curry leaves. When the mustard seeds splutter, add the onion. Sauté for a minute and mix in the green chillies.

Stir in the garlic and ginger and sprinkle in a little water. Add the spice powders, except the garam masala powder, and mix well.

Mix in the sprouts, salt and 3 cups of water and bring to a boil. Sprinkle in the garam masala powder and coriander leaves. Cover the pan and cook for 10-12 minutes.

To serve
Spoon a ladle of cooked sprouts into a deep bowl. Sprinkle generously with gram flour strings. Top with onion, coriander leaves and freshly squeezed lime juice. Serve with lime slices and pav on the side.

Mung Besan Chila (Mung and Gram Flour Pancakes)

4 servings

Filling
4 medium potatoes, boiled
  and peeled
1 tbsp ghee
1 tsp cumin seeds/jeera
1 medium onion, chopped
4 green chillies, chopped
1 tbsp chopped coriander
  leaves/hara dhania
½ tsp red chilli powder
1 tsp mango powder/amchur
1 tsp salt

Chila
1 cup husked mung beans/
  mung dal
4 green chillies, chopped
2 tbsp fresh yogurt/dahi
1 tbsp gram flour/besan
A pinch of asafoetida powder/
  hing
½ tsp baking powder
1 tsp salt
Oil for cooking

Filling
Mash the potatoes coarsely or cut into very small pieces.

Put the ghee in a pan over moderate heat. When hot, add the cumin seeds and onion and stir-fry for about 3 minutes.

Add the green chillies and fry for 1 minute.

Mix in the potatoes, coriander leaves, chilli and mango powders and salt. Mix well and cook for 1 minute.

Remove from heat and set aside to cool.

Chila
Wash the dal and soak it overnight in water or for at least 3-4 hours.

Rinse the dal, drain thoroughly and grind it with the green chillies, yogurt and about ⅓ cup of water.

Blend in the gram flour, asafoetida powder, baking powder and salt.

Heat a non-stick tava or griddle and spread a spoon of batter over it.

Spread a little filling on the chila and smear a little oil along the edges. Fold the chila in half and cook over moderate heat on both sides.

Repeat with the remaining batter and filling.

Serve hot.

Kuttu ka Meetha Chila (Sweet Buckwheat Flour Pancakes)

Makes 5-6 pancakes

1 cup buckwheat flour/kuttu
   ka atta
3 tbsp sugar
Oil for cooking

Sift the flour into a bowl and mix in the sugar. Gradually add about 1½ cups of water and mix to make a batter of pouring consistency.

Put a non-stick frying pan over moderate heat. When hot, pour in a ladle of batter and swirl the pan to cover the base. Drizzle a few drops of oil all around. Cook each side for 2-3 minutes till light golden on both sides.

Make all the chila in the same way.

Kuttu Pakoda (Buckwheat Fritters)

2 servings

½ cup buckwheat flour/kuttu
   ka atta
1 tsp table salt or rock salt
Oil for deep-frying
2 medium potatoes, cut into
   thin round slices
½ cup chopped (1" cubes)
   yellow pumpkin/kaddu

Sift the flour and salt into a bowl. Gradually add about ⅓ cup of water and mix to make a smooth batter.

Heat the oil in a kadhai or wok. Dip the potato slices into the batter and fry them in batches over moderate heat, till golden brown. Drain and place on kitchen paper to absorb excess oil.

Repeat with the pumpkin cubes.

Serve hot.

Toasted Amaranth Rolls

8 servings

3 tbsp honey
1½ tbsp oil or butter
1½ tsp salt (optional)
1½ tbsp active dry yeast
1 cup amaranth flour/ramdana
  ka atta
2¼ cups wholewheat flour/
  gehun ka atta + extra for
  rolling
2 tbsp butter
½ cup popped amaranth
  seeds/ramdana

Filling
3 tbsp seedless raisins/
  kishmish
3 tbsp chopped mixed nuts
1 tsp powdered cinnamon/
  dalchini
2 tsp dried orange or sweet
  lime peel

Mix the honey, 1½ tbsp of oil or butter, salt and yeast with 1½ cups of lukewarm water in a bowl.

Sift in both flours. Knead to prepare a smooth dough. Cover the dough with a damp cloth and set aside for 1 hour.

Mix all the filling ingredients in another bowl.

Roll the dough ¼" thick on a lightly floured surface. Spread 2 tbsp butter over the dough and sprinkle the filling on top.

Roll the dough into a cylinder and cut it into 2" long slices.

Place the slices, cut side down, close together on a lightly greased baking tray.

Sprinkle popped amaranth seeds on the rolls and bake in an oven preheated to 175°C-180°C for 30-40 minutes.

Serve hot with ice cream or at room temperature with cream.

Besan Ramdana Dhokla (Gram Flour Amaranth Flour Savouries)

6 servings

1 cup gram flour/besan
1 cup amaranth flour/ramdana
ka atta
1 tbsp Eno's fruit salt
1 tsp baking powder
1 tsp salt
1 tsp sugar
1 cup buttermilk/chaas or
2 tbsp yogurt/dahi +
¾ cup water
Red chilli powder for
sprinkling

Ground to a paste
½" piece ginger, roughly
chopped
5-6 garlic cloves, roughly
chopped
3 green chillies, roughly
chopped
1 tbsp water (if required)

Sift both the flours, fruit salt, baking powder and salt into a bowl. Mix in the sugar.

Pour in the buttermilk or diluted yogurt and mix well. Add some water if needed, to make a batter of pouring consistency.

Add the ginger-garlic paste and beat well.

Pour the batter into lightly greased thalis (flat metal plates with a low rim) or small bowls to come halfway up the sides.

Sprinkle chilli powder on top, and steam for about 10 minutes, till done.

Cut into diamond-shaped pieces or squares and serve hot with green chutney, or garlic chutney (page 143).

Biscuit Roti (Stuffed Fried Bread)

Makes 20 roti

4 cups super-refined wheat flour/maida + extra for rolling
1½ tsp salt
6 tsp ghee
Oil for deep-frying

Filling
1½" piece ginger, finely chopped
3 tbsp gram flour/besan
3 tbsp semolina/rava/sooji
2½ tsp salt
1 cup grated fresh coconut

Tempering
4 tsp oil
½ tsp mustard seeds/rai/sarson
1 tsp husked black gram/urad dal
2 dried red chillies
6 green chillies, slit
1 tsp asafoetida powder/hing, mixed with 2 tsp water
2 sprigs of curry leaves

Dough
Sift the flour and salt into a bowl. Rub in the ghee. Gradually add about ½ cup of water and knead to prepare a smooth dough.

Filling
Put the oil for tempering in a pan over moderate heat. When hot, add the mustard seeds. When they splutter, add the remaining tempering ingredients and fry for about 20 seconds.

Add the ginger, gram flour and semolina and fry for about 2 minutes, stirring continuously, till the semolina changes colour.

Sprinkle in about ¼ cup of water and add the salt and coconut. Cook for 5-6 minutes over low heat. Remove the pan from heat and set aside to cool.

To assemble the roti
Divide the dough and filling into 20 portions and roll into balls.

Flatten the dough balls lightly in the palm of your hand and place a portion of filling in the centre. Fold the dough over the filling to cover it completely and press the top to seal it, using a little water if required.

Roll each ball on a lightly floured surface into a 3"-4" round roti

Heat the oil for deep-frying in a kadhai or wok to smoking point. Lower the heat and fry the roti in batches, till golden brown and crisp.

Drain and place on kitchen paper to absorb excess oil.

Serve hot.

Methi Vada (Fenugreek Fritters)
2 servings

150 gms fenugreek leaves/
  methi
2 cups maize flour/makki ka
  atta
1 tsp turmeric powder/haldi
1 tsp red chilli powder
1 tsp cumin seeds/jeera
1 tsp ajwain
1 tsp grated ginger
1 tsp sesame seeds/til
1 tsp salt
6 tbsp sunflower oil

Pluck the fenugreek leaves and discard the stems. Wash the leaves in several changes of water and shake off any excess water. Chop the leaves.

Combine all the ingredients, except the oil, in a bowl and mix well.

Gradually add about 1 cup of water to make a thick batter of dropping consistency.

Put the oil in a frying pan over moderate heat. When hot, drop in small balls of batter with the help of a ladle and fry the vade in batches, till light brown. Turn over, cover the pan and allow them to cook in their own steam over low heat for a few minutes.

Drain and place on kitchen paper to absorb excess oil.

Serve hot.

Masala Vada (Spicy Bengal Gram Patties)

6 servings

1 cup husked Bengal gram/
  chana dal
½ cup finely chopped onions
½ cup finely chopped
  coriander leaves / hara
  dhania
½ cup finely chopped dill
  leaves/shepu/sua bhaji
½ cup chopped mint leaves/
  pudina
3-4 green chillies, finely
  chopped
½ tsp cumin seeds/jeera
1½ tsp salt
Oil for deep-frying

Wash the gram and soak it in water for around 3-4 hours. Drain and rinse thoroughly.

Reserve 2 tbsp of the gram and coarsely grind the rest.

Transfer the ground gram and the reserved gram to a bowl. Mix in the remaining ingredients, except the oil. Add 2-3 tbsp of hot oil and mix well.

Wet your hands and pinch off lemon-sized balls of the mixture. Flatten them into round patties or vade.

Put the oil in a kadhai or wok over moderate heat. When hot, fry the vade in batches on both sides, till golden brown. Drain and place on kitchen paper to absorb excess oil.

Serve hot with green chutney, date and tamarind chutney (page 143), or ketchup.

Khasta Kachori (Stuffed Fried Buns of Heaven)

Makes 15-16 kachori

Dough
4 cups super-refined wheat
  flour/maida
1 cup wholewheat flour/gehun
  ka atta
1 cup gram flour/besan
1 cup semolina/rava/sooji
2 tsp salt
1 tsp sodium bicarbonate
½ cup coriander seeds/dhania
¼ cup oil
Ghee for deep-frying

Filling
¼ cup black pepper powder/
  kali miri
1 cup powdered roasted
  fennel seeds/saunf
½ cup cumin powder/jeera
2 tsp red chilli powder
1 tsp garlic paste
1 tsp ginger paste

Syrup
¼ cup sugar
1 tbsp milk
2 saffron strands/kesar

Note

The unsweetened kachori may be stored without refrigeration for a week in an airtight container and sweetened when required.

Sift all the flours for the dough into a bowl. Add the remaining dough ingredients, except the ghee for frying, and mix well. Gradually add about 4 cups of water and knead to prepare a pliable dough. Cover with a damp cloth and set aside.

Mix the filling ingredients in another bowl. The mixture should be soft and crumbly. Set aside.

Combine the syrup ingredients, except the saffron, in a pan. Mix in 4 tbsp of water and boil till the syrup has a single thread consistency. (Hold a drop of cooled syrup between the thumb and index finger. Separate the fingers: a thread should be formed.) Strain and add the saffron. Set aside.

Divide the dough and filling into 15-16 equal portions.

Roll each portion of dough into a small round shape and place a portion of filling in the centre. Fold the dough over the filling to cover it completely, and press the top to seal it, using a little water if required. Shape into a round ball.

Put the ghee in a kadhai or wok over low heat. When hot, fry the kachori in batches, till light brown, turning once. Drain and place on kitchen paper to absorb excess ghee.

When cool enough to handle, make a hole in the centre of each kachori, about ½" in diameter, and pour about ½ tbsp of syrup into it. Roll the kachori around so that the syrup spreads. Allow to stand for 30 minutes before serving.

Khandvi (Gram Flour Rolls)

4 servings

¾ cup gram flour/besan
¾ cup fresh yogurt/dahi
½ tsp ginger paste
½ tsp green chilli paste
¼ tsp turmeric powder/haldi
A pinch of asafoetida powder/
  hing
¾ tsp salt

Tempering
2 tbsp oil
1 tsp mustard seeds/rai/
  sarson
1 tsp asafoetida powder/hing
3-4 curry leaves
4 dried red chillies

Garnish
2 tbsp grated fresh coconut
2 tbsp chopped coriander
  leaves/hara dhania

Sift the gram flour into a bowl Add the remaining ingredients, except the tempering and garnish. Pour in 1 cup of water. Whisk to make a smooth batter.

Transfer the batter to a non-stick pan and place it over low heat, stirring continuously to avoid lumps. Keep stirring till the batter becomes thick. Taste the batter to check if the gram flour is cooked. This will take about 7-10 minutes.

Spread the batter as thinly as possible on the reverse of a thali (a flat metal plate with a low rim), using your hands or a rubber spatula, while the batter is still hot. The number of plates you need depends on how thinly you can spread the batter.

When you finish spreading the batter on the last plate, return to the first one, and roll the firmed up batter carefully like a Swiss roll. Repeat with the other plates.

Cut each roll into 1" pieces to get bite-sized khandvi. Arrange them on a serving platter.

Put the oil for tempering in a small pan over moderate heat. When hot, add the remaining tempering ingredients. Stir for 30 seconds and pour the contents of the pan over the khandvi.

Garnish with coconut and coriander leaves and serve.

Shev (Gram Flour Strings)

5 servings

500 gms gram flour/besan
¼ tsp ajwain
½ tsp ginger-garlic paste
1 tsp salt
½ tsp red chilli powder
1 litre peanut oil for deep-
  frying

Sift the gram flour into a bowl. Add the remaining ingredients, except the oil, and mix well. Gradually add about 1 cup of water and mix to make a batter of pouring consistency.

Heat the oil in a kadhai or wok to smoking point. Reduce the heat to low.

Hold a metal strainer over the oil and pour a ladle of batter into it. Move the strainer around to spread the strands of batter in the oil. Separate the strands gently with a slotted spoon and fry till crisp and golden. Drain and place on kitchen paper to absorb excess oil.

Make the remaining shev in the same way.

Serve hot and crisp.

Chakli (Crisp-Fried Multigrain Spirals)

Makes 40 chakli

1 cup wholewheat flour/gehun ka atta
½ cup rice flour/chaval ka atta
½ cup super-refined wheat flour/maida
½ cup gram flour/besan
½ tsp red chilli powder
2 tsp white sesame seeds/til
2 tsp cumin seeds/jeera
3 tbsp butter
2 tsp salt
Butter paper or damp plastic sheet
Oil for deep-frying

Sift all the flours together into a bowl. Transfer to a muslin cloth and tie the ends of the cloth with a string.

Place the muslin bag in a steamer and steam for 20 minutes.

Beat the steamed flour with a wooden spoon to powder it. Sift the contents of the muslin bag into a bowl. Powder any lumps and sift again.

Add the remaining ingredients, except the butter paper or plastic sheet and oil, and mix well.

Gradually add about 2 cups of water and knead to prepare a soft but not sticky dough.

Place some dough in a chakli press or an icing bag with a star-shaped nozzle and make 3" discs of concentric circles touching each other, on a piece of butter paper or damp plastic sheet.

Put the oil in a kadhai or wok over moderate heat. When hot, fry the chakli in batches, till crisp and golden. Drain and place on kitchen paper to absorb excess oil.

Cool and store in an airtight container.

Breads

Roti (Wholewheat Bread)

Makes about 8 roti

- 1 cup wholewheat flour/gehun ka atta + extra for rolling
- 1 tsp salt
- 1 tsp ghee + extra for cooking

Sift the flour and salt into a bowl. Rub in 1 tsp of ghee till the mixture resembles breadcrumbs. Gradually add about ½ cup of hot water and knead well to prepare a soft pliable dough.

Cover the dough with a damp cloth and set aside to rest for 1 hour.

Knead the dough again for 1-2 minutes.

Pinch off golf-ball-sized portions of dough. Dust them with flour and roll into balls.

Roll out each ball of dough on a lightly floured surface into a 5" round roti.

Put a tava or griddle over moderate heat. When hot, smear it with ghee.

Roast both sides of roti on the tava or griddle till brown spots appear on the surface.

Cook all the rotis in the same way, greasing the tava or griddle as required.

Note

Roti can be stored in airtight containers in the freezer for up to 2 months. Just defrost before use.

Variation: To make **Phulka** (Puffed Wholewheat Bread), after the roti is ready, hold it with a pair of tongs, directly over the glowing embers of a coal fire or the flame of a gas burner. The roti will puff up and the phulka is ready. Usually ghee is spread over the phulka before serving. Serve immediately.

Paratha (Pan-Fried Flatbread)

Makes 4-5 paratha

1 cup wholewheat flour/gehun
  ka atta + extra for rolling
1 tsp salt
1 tsp ghee + extra for cooking
½ cup hot water

Prepare the dough as given for roti (page 123). Cover the dough with a damp cloth and set aside to rest for 1 hour.

Pinch off golf-ball-sized portions of dough. Dust with flour and roll into balls.

Roll out each ball on a lightly floured surface into a 2" round roti. Brush the top with ghee. Fold in half and then into a quarter. Roll out again into a 5" paratha.

Put a tava or griddle over moderate heat. When hot, smear it with ghee.

Roast a paratha on both sides till brown spots appear on the surface.

You could drizzle a few drops of ghee around the sides while cooking it if you prefer a crisp and richer paratha.

Cook all the paratha in the same way, greasing the tava or griddle as required.

Tandoori Roti

Makes 10-12 roti

2 cups slightly coarse
  wholewheat flour/gehun ka
  atta + extra for rolling
¼ cup super-refined wheat
  flour/maida
1 tsp salt
2 tbsp ghee
2 tbsp yogurt/dahi

Sift both the flours with the salt into a bowl. Mix in the ghee and then the yogurt.

Gradually add about 1 cup of water and knead to prepare a slightly stiff dough.

Cover and set aside for 2 hours.

Pinch off lemon-sized balls of dough and flatten them. Roll out each ball on a lightly floured surface into a ⅛" thick roti.

Heat a tava or griddle over moderate heat and place a roti on it. After about 20 seconds, moisten the top of the roti with water and turn it over.

Invert the tava or griddle over the flame. The roti will stick to the tava or griddle. Roast the roti over the flame. When done, the roti will fall off the tava or griddle.

Serve hot.

Naan

Makes 10-12 naan

2½ cups super-refined wheat flour/maida + extra for rolling
½ tsp sodium bicarbonate
½ tsp salt
1 tbsp poppy seeds/khus-khus
2 tbsp ghee + extra for cooking
¼ cup warm milk
½ cup buttermilk/chaas or 2 tsp yogurt/dahi + 8 tsp water

Sift the flour with the sodium bicarbonate and salt into a bowl.

Add the poppy seeds, 2 tbsp of ghee, milk and the buttermilk or diluted yogurt. Mix well and knead to prepare a firm dough. Sprinkle a little warm water if required and knead for 5-7 minutes. Set aside for 3 hours.

Roll out and cook the naan as given for roti (page 123).

Puri/Luchi (Deep-Fried Bread)

Makes 30-40 puri

2½ cups wholewheat flour/gehun ka atta
2½ tsp ghee
1 tsp salt
Peanut oil for deep-frying

Sift the flour into a bowl. Add the remaining ingredients, except the oil, and mix well.

Gradually add about ⅔ cup of water and knead for at least 10 minutes or longer to prepare an elastic dough.

Pinch off marble-sized balls of dough. Flatten the balls slightly between your palms Dip the balls in a little oil, to prevent them from sticking to the surface while rolling. Roll out into 4" round puri.

Heat the oil in a kadhai or wok till smoking. Lower the heat to moderate and fry the puri in batches.

Press the puri down with a spoon so that they are below the surface of the oil, to puff up. Turn over and fry for 1 minute. The colour should be beige. Remove from pan, drain and place on kitchen paper to absorb excess oil.

Bhature (Leavened Deep-Fried Bread)

Makes 8-10 bhature

1 cup semolina/rava/sooji
2 cups super-refined wheat
  flour/maida
½ tsp sodium bicarbonate
½ tsp salt
½ tsp sugar
½ cup sour yogurt/dahi
Oil for deep-frying

Soak the semolina in just enough water to cover for 10 minutes.

Sift the flour, sodium bicarbonate and salt into a bowl. Mix in the semolina, sugar and yogurt.

Gradually add about 1 cup of warm water and knead to prepare a soft, elastic dough. Knead again with greased hands till the dough is smooth.

Brush the dough with oil and place it in a bowl. Cover the bowl with a damp cloth or cling film and set aside in a warm place for 3-4 hours.

Divide the dough into 8-10 balls. Roll out each ball into an oval.

Put the oil in a kadhai or wok over moderate heat. When hot, fry each bhatura separately, till golden. Drain and place on kitchen paper to absorb excess oil.

Serve hot with Pindi chhole (page 48).

Kulcha (Baked Leavened Bread)

Makes 8 kulcha

4 cups super-refined wheat
flour/maida + extra for
rolling
1 tsp salt
1 tsp baking powder
2 tbsp yogurt/dahi
1 tsp sugar
1 tbsp oil
¼ cup ghee

Sift the flour, salt, and baking powder into a bowl. Mix the yogurt with the sugar and 1 cup of warm water in another bowl and pour it into the bowl containing the flour. Mix to prepare a dough and knead it for 10-15 minutes.

Gather the dough to form a ball. Lightly oil the ball. Cover with a damp cloth or cling film and set aside to rest for about 2 hours.

Knead the dough again for about 5 minutes.

Divide the dough into 8 balls.

Place a ball of dough on a lightly floured surface and flatten it. Roll out the dough into a round, or oval shape, about ¼" thick.

Make the remaining kulcha in the same way. Brush the kulcha with ghee and place them on a lightly greased baking sheet. Bake in an oven preheated to 240°C for about 8 minutes.

Serve hot.

Jowar ki Roti (Sorghum Bread)

Makes 4 roti

1 cup sorghum flour/jowar ka
  atta
1 tbsp oil
1 green chilli, finely chopped
½ tsp salt to taste

Sift the flour into a bowl. Add the remaining ingredients and mix well.

Gradually add about ¼ cup of warm water and knead to prepare a soft dough. Cover and set aside for 10 minutes.

Divide the dough into 4 equal portions.

Pat each portion on a dry surface using your palm to make a 5" round roti.

Put a tava or griddle over moderate heat. When hot, roast each roti on both sides till lightly browned.

Serve hot.

Jowar Bhakri (Sorghum Bread)

Makes 2 bhakri

1 cup sorghum flour/jowar ka
  atta (freshly ground) +
  extra for rolling
A pinch of salt

Sift the flour and salt into a bowl. Gradually add about ¾ cup of water and keep mixing till the flour can be gathered up into a ball of dough.

Knead the dough gently on a lightly floured surface, for a minute or so.

Divide the dough into 2 portions. Lightly flour your hands and shape each portion into a thick disc, flattening it with your fingertips and between the palms of your hands. Place the bhakri on a lightly floured surface and continue to shape it, pressing it out with your fingertips, till you have an 8" round bhakri.

Put a tava or griddle over low heat. When hot, put a bhakri on it. After a few minutes the bhakri will start getting opaque. Sprinkle some water on the surface with your fingers. After about 2 minutes turn the bhakri over and cook on the other side for another 2 minutes.

Turn the bhakri twice till it develops brown spots all over and becomes lighter in colour.

Serve hot with butter.

Note

If the flour is not freshly ground, the dough starts cracking at the edges, so freshly ground sorghum flour is absolutely necessary.

Ragi Roti (Finger Millet Bread)

Makes 10-12 roti

2 cups finger millet flour/ragi/
nachni ka atta
¾ cup wholewheat flour/
gehun ka atta + extra for
rolling

Sift both the flours into a bowl. Gradually add about ½ cup of water and knead to prepare a stiff dough.

Divide the dough into 10-12 balls and roll out into 5" round roti, on a lightly floured surface.

Put a tava or griddle over low heat. When hot, put a roti on it and roast on both sides, till reddish brown spots appear on the surface.

Bajra Bhakri (Pearl Millet Bread)

Makes 10-12 bhakri

3 cups pearl millet flour/bajra
ka atta
1 cup wholewheat flour/gehun
ka atta + extra for rolling

Sift both the flours into a bowl. Gradually add about 1 cup of water and knead to prepare a stiff dough.

Divide the dough into 10-12 even-sized balls.

Roll out each ball on a lightly floured surface into a 4" round bhakri.

Put a tava or griddle over moderate heat. When hot, put a bhakri on it. Cook it on both sides till brown spots appear on the surface.

Pearl Millet Muffins

Makes about 12 muffins

1½ cups pearl millet flour/
   bajra ka atta
½ cup soy flour/bhatt ka atta
1 tbsp baking powder
½ tsp salt (optional)
¼ tsp orange flavouring
   (commercial, optional)
1 cup water or orange juice
¼ cup oil
¼ cup honey

Sift all the dry ingredients into a bowl and mix well.

Combine the remaining ingredients in another bowl. Mix well and pour it into the bowl containing the dry ingredients. Blend the ingredients well.

Spoon the mixture into well-greased muffin tins.

Bake in the centre of an oven preheated to 180°C for 15-20 minutes. Test if done by inserting a thin skewer into the centre of a muffin: it should come out clean. Bake for a little longer if necessary.

Turn the muffins out on to a wire rack to cool.

Methi na Dhebra (Fenugreek Bread)

4 servings

2 cups finely chopped
  fenugreek leaves/methi
1 cup millet flour/bajra ka atta
¼ cup wholewheat flour/
  gehun ka atta + extra for
  rolling
1 tbsp gram flour/besan
½ tsp red chilli powder
¼ tsp asafoetida powder/hing
¼ tsp semolina/rava/sooji
½ cup fresh yogurt/dahi
2 tbsp finely chopped garlic
2 green chillies, chopped
1 tsp sugar
1½ tsp salt
1 tbsp oil + extra for frying

Combine all the ingredients, except the oil for frying, and knead to prepare a soft dough, adding a little water if required.

Pinch off lime-sized balls of dough and roll out into 4" round dhebra, on a lightly floured surface.

Put a tava or griddle over moderate heat. When hot, put a dhebra on it and cook on both sides, drizzling a little oil around the edges, till golden brown spots appear on the surface.

Variation: Smaller, bite-sized dhebra can be made, 1½" in diameter and deep-fried in hot oil till golden brown.

Ramdana Roti (Amaranth Flatbread)

Makes 6 roti

1½ cups amaranth flour/
ramdana ka atta
1 cup wholewheat flour/gehun
ka atta + extra for rolling

Sift both the flours into a bowl. Gradually add about ¾ cup of water and knead to prepare a stiff dough.

Divide the dough into 6 balls and roll them out into 4" round roti on a lightly floured surface.

Put a tava or griddle over low heat. When hot, put a roti on it and roast on both sides till brown spots appear on the surface.

Amaranth Bread

Makes 8 servings

1 cup amaranth flour/ramdana
ka atta
1½ cup wholewheat flour/
gehun ka atta or rice flour/
chaval ka atta
1 tbsp baking powder
1 tsp salt (optional)
1 cup milk or water
3 tbsp honey
2 tbsp oil + extra for greasing
2 egg whites (if using rice
flour)

Sift the dry ingredients together into a bowl.

Mix the milk or water, honey and 2 tbsp of oil in another bowl and stir it into the dry ingredients.

Whisk the egg whites till stiff peaks form when the whisk is raised. Fold them gently into the batter (if using rice flour).

Pour the batter into a well-greased 8" x 4" loaf tin.

Bake in the centre of an oven preheated to 175°-180°C for about 45 minutes. Test if done by inserting a thin skewer into the centre of the loaf: it should come out clean. Bake for a little longer if necessary.

Switch off the oven and leave the loaf inside the oven for 10 minutes.

Turn the loaf out on to a wire rack to cool.

Kuttu aur Alu ka Paratha (Buckwheat and Potato Pan-Fried Flatbread)

Makes 4-5 paratha

1 cup buckwheat flour/kuttu
   ka atta
1 medium potato, boiled,
   peeled and mashed
¼ tsp ajwain
⅓ tsp salt
Green chillies to taste,
   chopped
Ghee or oil to cook paratha
   (optional)

Sift the flour into a bowl. Mix in the potato, ajwain, salt and green chillies. Gradually add about ⅓ cup of water and knead well to prepare a smooth dough.

Divide the dough into 4-5 portions. Roll each portion of dough into a 4" round paratha.

Put a tava or griddle over moderate heat. When hot, put a paratha on it and roast on both sides till brown spots appear on the surface.

You could drizzle a few drops of ghee or oil around the sides while cooking it if you prefer a crisp and richer paratha.

Make all the paratha in the same way.

Makki ki Roti (Maize Flour Bread)

Makes 8 roti

1 cup maize flour/makki ka
   atta
¼ cup wholewheat flour/
   gehun ka atta
1 green chilli, finely chopped
¾ tsp salt
1 tsp oil

Combine all the ingredients, except the oil, in a bowl. Gradually add about ⅓ cup of water and knead well to prepare a soft dough.

Divide the dough into 6 equal portions. Roll out each portion between two plastic sheets into a 4" round roti.

Put a non-stick tava or griddle over moderate heat. When hot, put a roti on it and roast on both sides, using very little oil, till brown spots appear on the surface.

Serve hot.

Appa (Kerala Rice Bread)

Makes 6 appa

¼ tsp salt
2 cups rice flour/chaval ka
   atta

Boil 1 cup of water with the salt. Add the flour and stir till all the water is absorbed. Remove from heat and set aside till cool enough to handle.

Knead to prepare a soft dough, adding a little water if required.

Divide the dough into 6 balls.

Sprinkle a little water on a wooden board. Wet your hand and press each ball on the board evenly, to make a round roti.

Put an earthen tava or griddle over moderate heat. Lower the heat and put a roti on it. When the edges start to curl upwards, flip the roti over to cook the other side. As it rises, press the edges till it puffs up like a ball.

Transfer to a plate lined with a paper napkin. Make the remaining roti in the same way.

Accompaniments

Horse Gram Salad

4 servings

½ cup horse gram sprouts/
  kulthi ka dal/gahath
1 medium tomato
100 gms firm cottage cheese/
  paneer, cut into 2" sticks
1 medium onion, finely sliced
1 capsicum/Shimla mirch,
  finely slivered
1 carrot, finely slivered
1 spring onion, finely chopped
1 tsp finely chopped coriander
  leaves/hara dhania
¼ tsp crushed dried red
  chillies
½ tsp cumin seeds/jeera,
  crushed
1 tsp white vinegar

Marinade
1 tbsp white vinegar
1 tsp olive oil
¼ tsp freshly ground black
  pepper/kali miri
½ tsp sugar
A sprig of fresh dill leaves/
  shepu/sua bhaji (optional)
2-3 fresh mint leaves/pudina
1 tsp sugar, crushed
½ tsp salt

Pressure-cook the horse gram sprouts with about ½ cup of water for 10 minutes after the cooker reaches full pressure.

Drain, rinse under running cold water, and set aside in a colander.

Combine all marinade ingredients in a bowl and mix well.

Cut the tomato in half, scoop out the pulp and seeds with a spoon and stir it into the marinade. Slice the tomato shells into fine slivers.

Add the paneer sticks to the marinade and toss gently till well-coated. Set aside to marinate for 30 minutes.

Transfer the paneer and marinade to a large glass bowl. Mix in the remaining ingredients.

Chill well before serving.

Sprout and Peanut Salad

2 servings

½ cup peanuts
½ cup sprouted mung beans
½ cup sprouted whole Bengal
  gram/kala chana
1 lime, juice extracted
½ tsp salt
¼ tsp freshly ground black
  pepper/kali miri

Garnish
2 tbsp chopped coriander
  leaves/hara dhania
  (optional)

Roast the peanuts and remove the skin.

Mix the peanuts with the sprouts in a bowl. Sprinkle in the lime juice, salt and pepper. Toss gently till the salad is well coated with the seasonings.

Garnish with coriander leaves (if used) and serve chilled.

Onion Pachadi (Onion Relish)

2 servings

½ tbsp oil
2 large onions, sliced
6 green chillies, chopped
½ cup grated fresh coconut,
  ground
½ cup yogurt/dahi, whisked
½ tsp salt

Tempering
½ tbsp oil
½ tsp husked black gram/
  urad dal
½ tsp mustard seeds/rai/
  sarson
5 curry leaves

Garnish
2 tsp chopped coriander
  leaves/hara dhania

Put the oil in a pan over moderate heat. When hot, add the onions and fry till soft. Remove from heat and add the green chillies and coconut to the pan.

Mix in the yogurt and salt.

Put the oil for tempering in a small pan over moderate heat. When hot, add the remaining tempering ingredients. When the mustard seeds splutter, mix the contents of the pan into the pachadi.

Garnish with coriander leaves and serve with Kannadiga tomato pulao (page 95).

Rasam (Pepper Water)

4 servings

2 tbsp pigeon peas/tuvar dal/
  arhar dal
1½ tsp tamarind soaked in
  ¼ cup water
1 small tomato, chopped
2-3 tsp rasam powder
  (commercial)
A pinch of asafoetida powder/
  hing
A pinch of turmeric powder/
  haldi
1 tsp salt

Tempering
1 tsp oil
¼ tsp mustard seeds/rai/
  sarson
5-6 curry leaves

Garnish
1 tbsp chopped coriander
  leaves

Wash the dal and pressure-cook it with 1 cup of water for 10 minutes after the cooker reaches full pressure. Open the cooker when cool.

Extract the tamarind pulp, add it to the cooker with the tomato and simmer for 2-3 minutes.

Sprinkle in the spice powders, salt and 3 cups of water and simmer for 8-10 minutes.

Put the oil for tempering in a small pan over moderate heat. When hot, add the mustard seeds and curry leaves. When the mustard seeds splutter, pour the contents of the pan into the rasam.

Simmer for another 4-5 minutes.

Serve hot, garnished with coriander leaves.

Dahi Bhalle (Lentil Dumplings in Spiced Yogurt)

6 servings

Dumplings
1½ cups husked black gram/
    urad dal
1 medium onion, finely
    chopped
1" piece ginger, chopped
2 tbsp chopped coriander
    leaves/hara dhania
2 green chillies, chopped
½ tsp cumin seeds/jeera
½ tsp salt
¼ tsp sodium bicarbonate
Oil for deep-frying

Spiced yogurt
15-20 seedless raisins/
    kishmish
3 cups yogurt/dahi, whisked
1 tsp salt
½ tsp cumin powder/jeera

Garnish
½ tsp red chilli powder
1 tbsp chopped coriander
    leaves/hara dhania
½ tsp coarsely ground cumin
    seeds/jeera

Wash the gram and soak it in water for 3 hours. Drain, rinse and drain again thoroughly.

Grind it to a coarse batter with the remaining dumpling ingredients, except the oil.

Moisten your hands and shape the batter into 2" round dumplings.

Put the oil in a kadhai or wok over moderate heat. When hot, fry the dumplings in batches, till light brown.

Drain and place them in a large bowl of hot water for 10 minutes.

Soak the raisins in water for 10 minutes. Drain and add them to the yogurt with the salt and cumin powder.

Squeeze the water from the dumplings and arrange them on a flat serving dish. Pour the yogurt over them.

Garnish with chilli powder, coriander leaves and cumin.

Serve chilled or at room temperature with date and tamarind chutney (page 143).

Date and Tamarind Chutney

Makes about 50 gms of chutney

A golf-ball-sized piece of tamarind, without seeds and strings
30 gms dates/khajur
4 tsp sugar
1 tsp salt
½ tsp red chilli powder
½ tsp cumin powder/jeera
1 tsp black salt/kala namak

Soak the tamarind and dates in water for about 10 minutes. Drain and remove the date seeds.

Boil the tamarind, dates, sugar and salt with about 1½ cups of water for 5 minutes.

Blend the mixture in a mixer and strain. Add the remaining ingredients and mix well.

Refrigerate till required.

Lassun Chutney (Garlic Chutney)

Makes about 100 gms of chutney

4-5 garlic cloves
2 tsp oil
½ cup grated fresh coconut
4-5 dried red chillies
A marble-sized ball of tamarind
1 tsp salt

If the garlic cloves are large chop them roughly. Heat the oil and fry the garlic till brown.

Grind the fried garlic with the remaining ingredients, gradually adding 2-3 tsp of water.

Refrigerate till required.

Green Chutney

Makes about 250 gms of chutney

2 tsp oil
3-4 green chillies
½ cup grated fresh coconut
5-6 curry leaves
¼ cup coriander leaves/hara dhania
2-3 garlic cloves
¼ cup roasted Bengal gram/ bhuna chana
¼ tsp tamarind paste
1 tsp salt

Heat the oil in a pan and fry the green chillies over low heat.

Grind them along with the remaining ingredients, gradually adding 2-3 tsp of water.

Refrigerate till required.

Kari Patta Podi (Curry Leaf Chutney Powder)

Makes about 200 gms of podi

½ cup grated dried coconut/
  kopra
¼ cup roasted Bengal gram/
  bhuna chana
25 curry leaves
2 dried red chillies
1 tsp mustard seeds/rai/
  sarson
½ tsp tamarind paste
1 tsp salt

Roast the coconut, gram, curry leaves, red chillies and mustard seeds separately in a pan over moderate heat for 2-3 minutes, stirring continuously, till crisp

Grind the roasted ingredients with the remaining ingredients to a coarse powder.

Store in an airtight container.

Chira Bhaja

Missal Pav

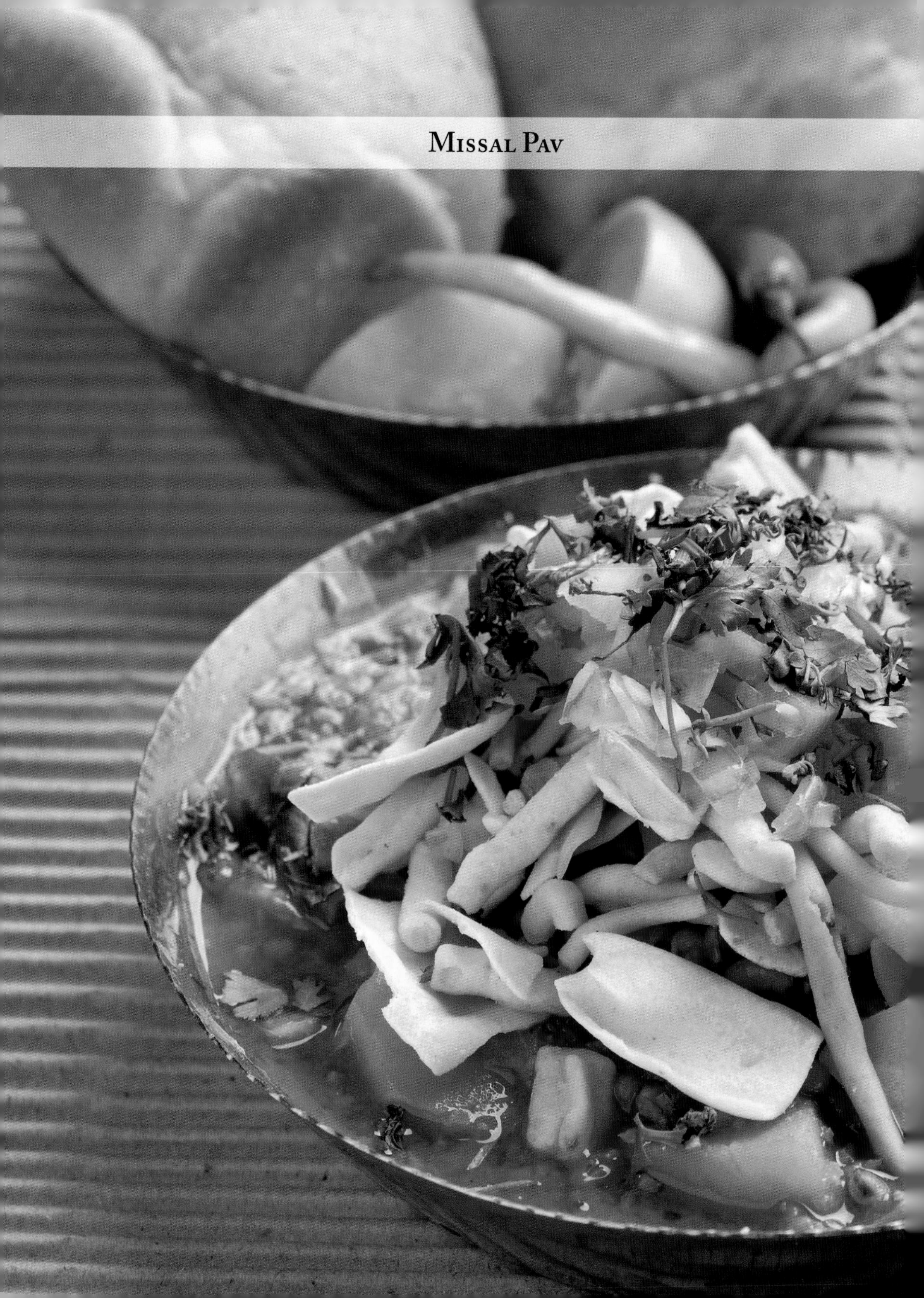

Puri / Luchi

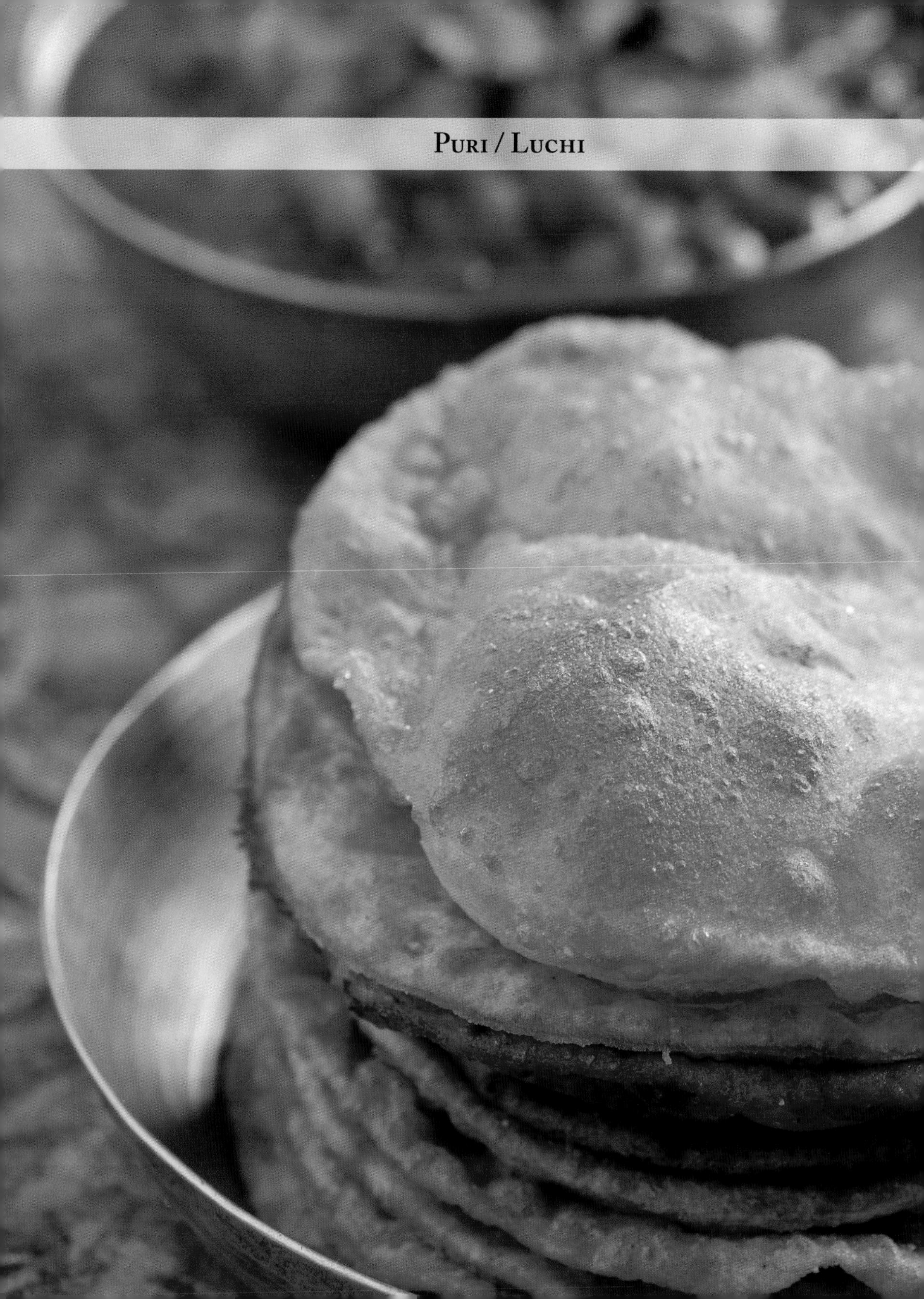

Modak

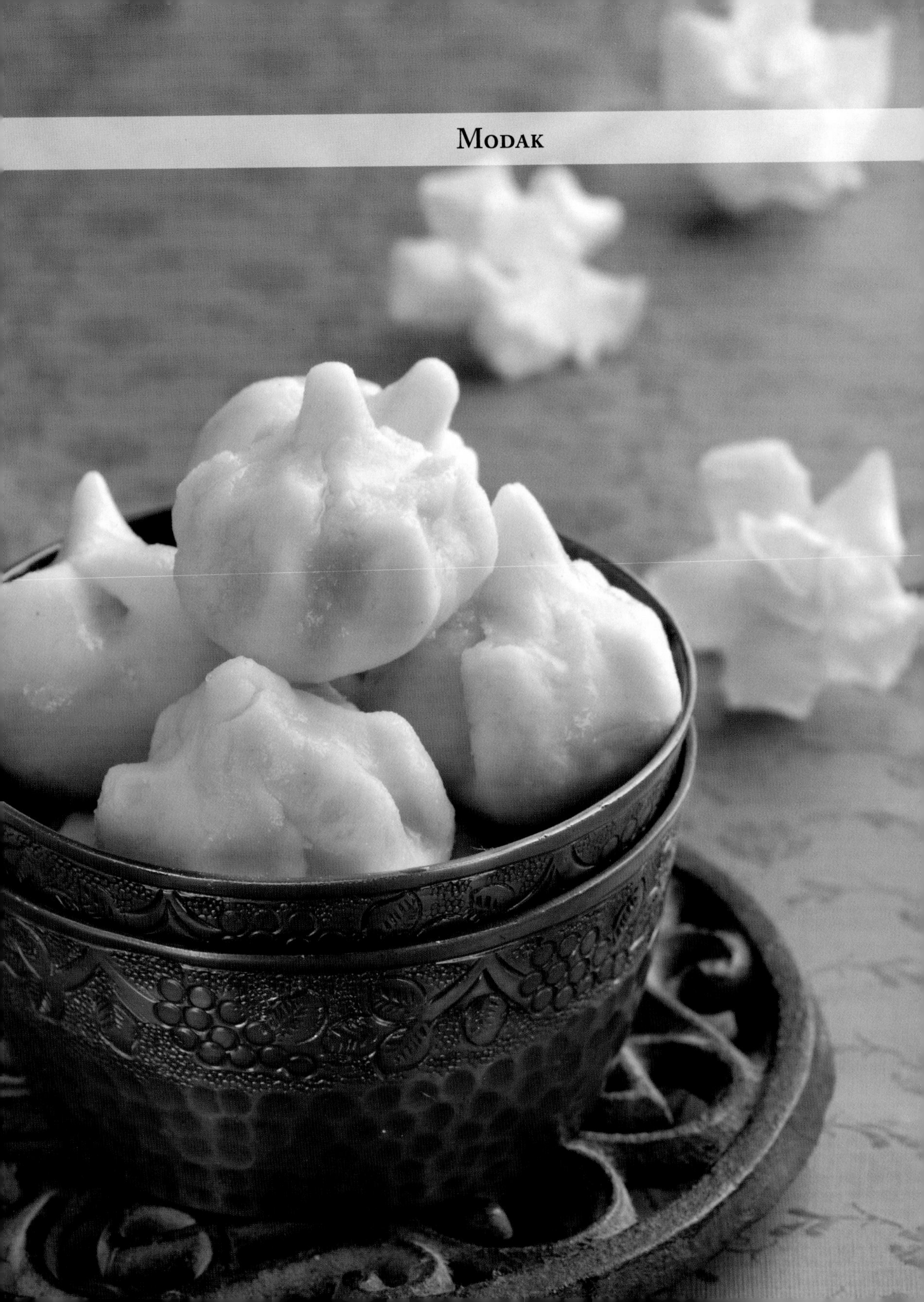

Gehun Laddu

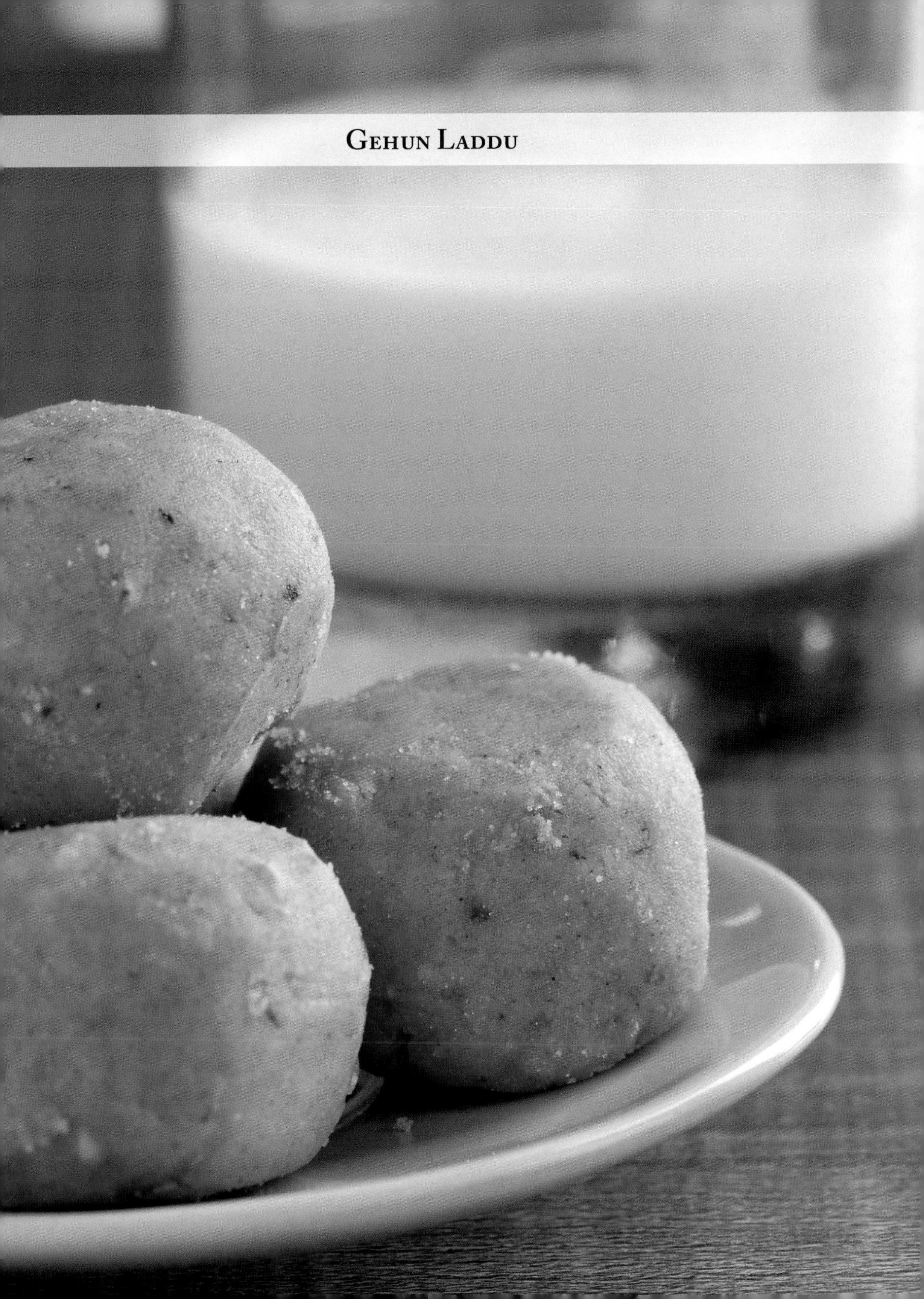

Jhangora Phirni

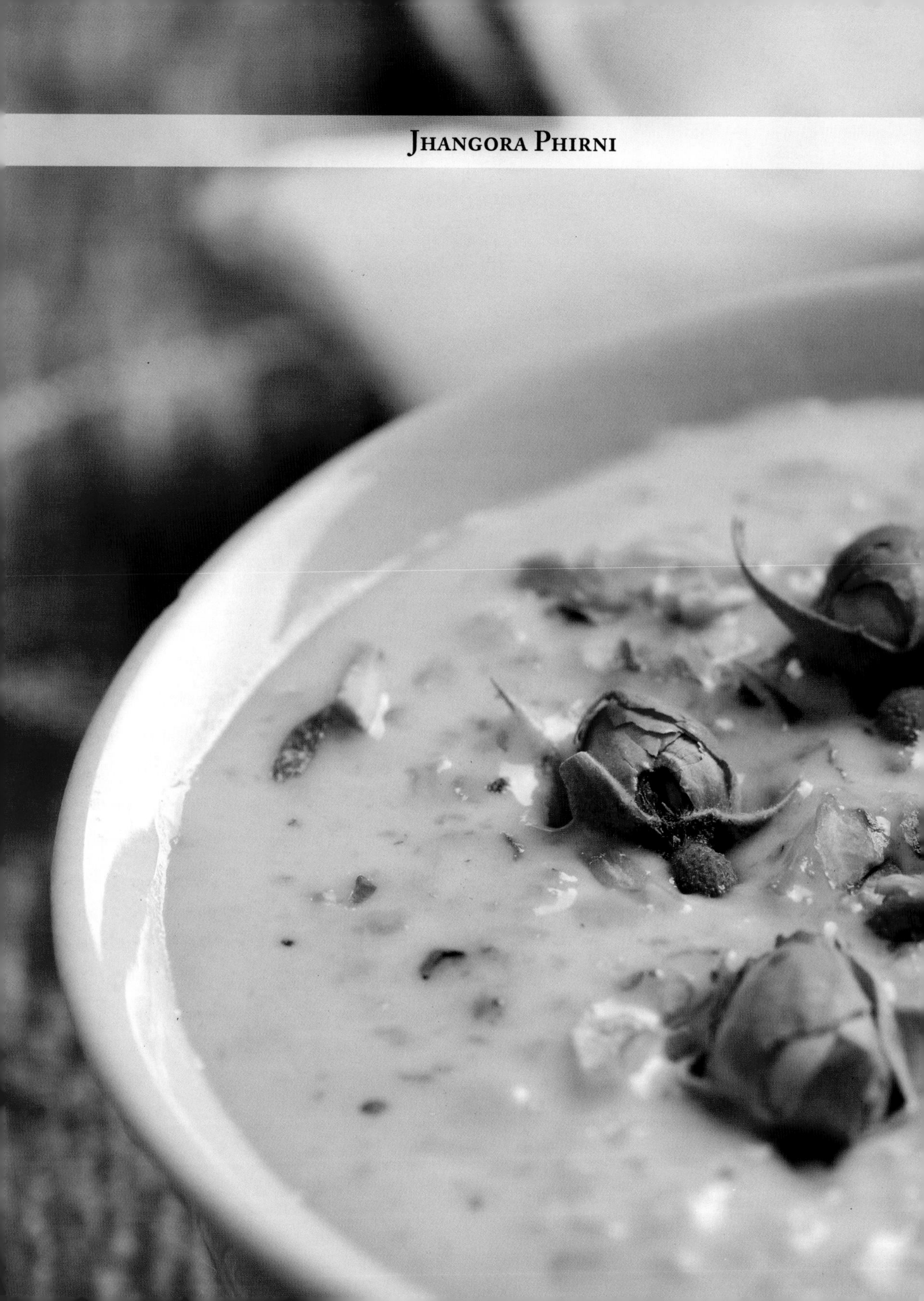

Shrikand

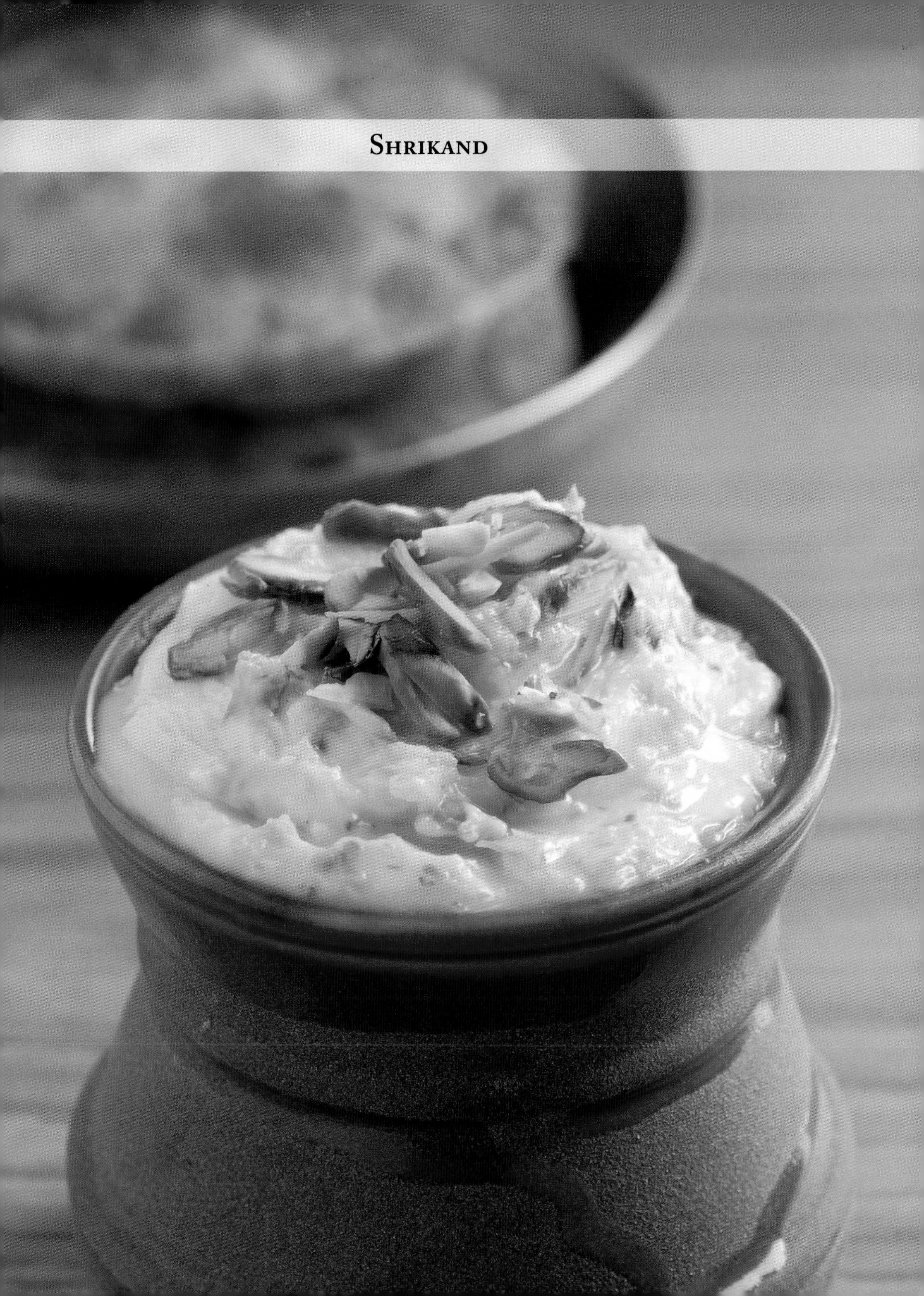

Desserts and Sweets

Kadhailyan (Rice Flour Dessert)

8-10 servings

1 cup grated fresh coconut
1 cup grated jaggery/gud
½ cup cashew nuts (optional)
½ cup fine rice flour/
 chaval ka atta
1 tsp powdered green
 cardamom/chhoti elaichi

Grind the coconut with ½ cup of water and press out the milk into a bowl, through a strainer lined with muslin.

Place the jaggery and cashew nuts (if used) with ½ cup of water in a pan and cook over low heat for 10 minutes.

Mix the rice flour with a little water to make a fine paste.

Pour the rice paste slowly into the jaggery syrup, stirring continuously to avoid lumps. Cook for 4-5 minutes, stirring all the while.

Mix in the coconut milk and cardamom.

Bring to a boil, stirring continuously, and remove from heat immediately.

Serve hot or chilled.

Jeebrutee Kheer (Rice Ball and Coconut Dessert)

8-10 servings

Jeebrutee (rice balls)
1½ cups uncooked rice
½ cup beaten rice/poha
½ fresh coconut, grated
Ghee for deep-frying

Kheer
1½ fresh coconuts, grated
2 cups grated jaggery/gud
10 green cardamoms/
   chhoti elaichi, powdered

Jeebrutee
Wash the uncooked rice. Drain and soak it with the beaten rice in 2 cups of water for 2 hours.

Drain the rice and grind it with the coconut to make a fine paste.

Transfer to a pan and add 3 cups of water. Put it over low heat and cook for 8-10 minutes, stirring all the while, till the mixture thickens into a dough that can be shaped into balls.

When the dough is cool enough to handle, rub a little ghee on your fingers and make small balls the size of large beads or jeebrutee.

Heat the ghee in a kadhai or wok over moderate heat and deep-fry the jeebrutee in batches, till reddish brown. Drain and place on kitchen paper to absorb excess ghee. (They may be steamed for 10 minutes if preferred.)

Kheer
Grind the coconut with 3-4 cups of water and press out the milk into a bowl, through a strainer lined with muslin.

Combine the jaggery with ½ cup of water in a pan and stir over moderate heat to make a syrup. As the syrup comes to a boil add the jeebrutee. Boil for about 5 minutes.

Mix in the coconut milk and cardamoms and remove from heat.

Serve hot or chilled.

Chakra Pongal (Sweet Rice)

6-8 servings

¾ cup husked mung beans/
   mung dal
2 cups rice
3 cups milk
3 cups grated jaggery/gud
½ cup ghee
½ cup cashew nuts
½ cup seedless raisins/
   kishmish
½ fresh coconut, grated
7-8 green cardamoms/chhoti
   elaichi, powdered

Wash the dal and rice separately.

Drain the dal thoroughly and roast lightly on a dry tava or griddle for 5-7 minutes, till you get the aroma of roasted mung.

Put the milk with 1 cup of water in a large pan over moderate heat and bring it to a boil. Add the dal and rice. Cook over low heat, till the liquid is absorbed and the dal and rice are soft and pulpy.

Mix in the jaggery and cook over low heat, stirring frequently to prevent the pongal from sticking to the base. (Adding about 4 tsp of ghee helps to prevent sticking.)

Remove from heat when the jaggery is blended in and the pongal has a sticky consistency.

Put 1 tbsp of ghee in a pan over moderate heat. When hot, add the cashew nuts, raisins and coconut and fry till the coconut is light golden. Sprinkle in the cardamoms, fry for a few seconds longer and pour the contents of the pan into the pongal.

Melt the remaining ghee and pour it into the pongal. Mix well.

Serve hot.

Inipu Idli (Sweet Steamed Rice Cakes)

Makes about 15 idli

1 cup uncooked rice
1 cup beaten rice/poha
1 cup grated fresh coconut
1 cup buttermilk/chaas or
  2 tbsp yogurt/dahi +
  ¾ cup water
½ cup grated jaggery/gud
4 green cardamoms/chhoti
  elaichi
7-8 cashew nuts, chopped
8-10 seedless raisins/
  kishmish
½ tsp salt
4 tbsp ghee

Wash the rice and drain it well. Dry it by spreading it on a piece of cloth for about an hour.

Grind the rice coarsely and transfer it to a bowl.

Grind the beaten rice, coconut and buttermilk or diluted yogurt to a smooth batter. Add the jaggery and cardamoms and grind till well blended.

Transfer the batter to the bowl containing the rice and mix well.

Stir in the cashew nuts and raisins. Add salt and mix well. Set aside for 4-5 hours.

Beat the batter well for a couple of minutes till light and frothy.

Grease the depressions of an idli mould with ghee and fill them with the batter. Steam the idli in a pressure cooker without the weight on for 8-10 minutes.

Serve hot.

Kesar Bhath (Saffron-Flavoured Sweet Rice)

10-12 servings

2 cups rice
½ cup ghee
4 cloves/lavang
2" stick cinnamon/dalchini
½ tsp saffron strands/kesar
  soaked in 1 tsp warm milk
3-4 cups sugar
6 green cardamoms/chhoti
  elaichi, powdered
½ tsp nutmeg powder/jaiphal
10 almonds, blanched peeled
  and slivered
1¼ cup seedless raisins/
  kishmish
½ lime, juice extracted

Wash the rice, drain well and spread out on a cloth to dry for 30-40 minutes.

Heat a little of the measured ghee in a large pan over low heat and toss in the cloves and cinnamon.

Add the rice and stir till it turns opaque. Pour in 3½ cups of hot water and cook till the rice is tender and the grains are separate.

Pour in the saffron with its soaking liquid.

Add the remaining ingredients and mix well. Cook over low heat till the rice is dry. Serve hot.

Phirni (Rice Custard)

6-8 servings

4 tbsp rice
1 litre milk
¾ cup sugar
½ tsp powdered green
    cardamom/chhoti elaichi

Decoration
8-10 almonds, blanched,
    peeled and slivered

Wash the rice and soak it in water for 1 hour. Drain the rice well and grind it to a coarse paste without any water.

Transfer it to a bowl and mix in ½ cup of water. Put the milk in a pan over moderate heat. Bring it to a boil and slowly add the rice paste, stirring continuously to avoid lumps.

Simmer for 5 minutes, stirring continuously. It should have the thick consistency of a custard.

Add the sugar and cardamoms, and simmer till the sugar dissolves, stirring all the while.

Remove from heat and pour the contents of the pan into an earthenware serving dish. Set aside till cool.

Sprinkle the almonds on top. Serve at room temperature or chilled.

Basundi (Rich Spiced Milk)

About 6 servings

4 litres milk
1-1½ cups sugar
½ tsp powdered green
  cardamom/chhoti elaichi
¼ tsp nutmeg powder/jaiphal
½ tbsp blanched, peeled and
  chopped almonds
½ tbsp chopped pistachios/
  pista

Place the milk in a pan over moderate heat and bring it to a boil. Continue boiling, stirring occasionally, till it is thick and reduced to ¾-1 litre.

Add the sugar and bring the milk to a boil. Lower the heat and simmer till the milk thickens again.

Stir in the spices and nuts and remove from heat.

Serve hot or chilled.

Mung Bean Dessert

8 servings

1 tbsp ghee
2 cups husked mung beans/
  mung dal
1½ cups grated jaggery/gud
3 cups coconut milk extracted
  from 1 coconut
½ tsp powdered green
  cardamom/chhoti elaichi

Heat the ghee in a heavy-based pan over moderate heat and roast the dal till you get the aroma of roasted mung.

Pour in 6 cups of water and cook till the dal is tender.

Stir in the jaggery and cook for 10 minutes.

Add the coconut milk and cardamom, give it a stir and remove from heat.

Serve hot or chilled.

Modak (Coconut and Jaggery-Filled Rice Dumplings)

Makes 20-24 dumplings

1½ cups parboiled rice/ukda/
   sela chaval
½ tsp ghee
A pinch of salt
Oil for greasing hands

Filling
1½ cups grated fresh coconut
¾ cup grated jaggery/gud
½ tsp powdered green
   cardamom/chhoti elaichi

Wash the rice and soak it in water for about 15 minutes. Drain well and spread out on a clean piece of cloth for an hour to dry.

Grind the rice fine. Run the ground rice through a sieve.

Boil 1¼ cups of water in a pan over moderate heat. Add the ghee and salt.

Slowly sprinkle in the ground rice, stirring continuously to avoid lumps. Cook over low heat, stirring continuously, till the mixture thickens to a semi-solid consistency. Remove from heat and keep covered for 15 minutes or till cool enough to handle.

Spread a little oil on your palms and knead the dough till soft and pliable. Cover with a damp cloth and set aside.

Mix the coconut and jaggery in a pan. Place it over low heat for 1-2 minutes, till the mixture turns golden. Stir in the cardamom.

Remove from heat and set aside till cool.

Make large, marble-sized balls of dough and flatten each into a 2" disc. Place a spoon of filling in the centre of each disc. Fold the dough over the filling to cover it completely, and press the top to seal it, using a little water if required. Shape into a round ball that has a peak on top, to resemble a fig.

Steam the modak in a steamer for 10 minutes.

Serve hot with ghee.

Note

These modak are prepared for Ganpathi puja.

Amaranth Fruitcake

10-12 servings

½ cup amaranth flour/
   ramdana ka atta
½ cup seedless dates/khajur,
   chopped
¼ cup figs/anjeer, chopped
2 egg whites
2 tsp honey
¼ cup butter or margarine
2 cups wholewheat flour/
   gehun ka atta
2 tsp baking powder
¼ cup chopped pineapple
½ cup walnuts, chopped
½ cup almonds, blanched,
   peeled and chopped
1 tsp vanilla extract

Sift the amaranth flour into a bowl. Add the dates and figs and pour in 1 cup of boiling water. Mix and set aside.

Beat the egg whites in a large bowl till stiff peaks form when the whisk is raised. Mix in the honey and butter or margarine and beat well. Sift in the wheat flour with the baking powder and fold it in.

Add the remaining ingredients, including the soaked amaranth and dried fruit, and mix well.

Pour the batter into a lightly greased loaf tin.

Bake in an oven preheated to 175°-180°C for 1¼ hours. Test if done by inserting a thin skewer into the centre of the cake: it should come out clean. Bake for a few minutes longer if necessary.

Turn the cake out on to a wire rack to cool.

Amaranth Apple Bake

6-8 servings

8 apples, chopped without
  peeling
¼ cup amaranth flour/
  ramdana ka atta
½ cup arrowroot powder/
  paniphal
1 tbsp honey
1 tsp powdered cinnamon/
  dalchini
2 tbsp popped amaranth
  seeds/ramdana

Place the apples in a pan with ¼ cup of water over moderate heat and cook till they are soft. Drain, peel and mash.

Sift the amaranth flour and arrowroot into the mashed apple and fold them in.

Add the honey and cinnamon and mix well.

Spoon the batter into a lightly greased baking dish. Sprinkle the popped amaranth on top.

Bake in an oven preheated to 175°-180°C for 20 minutes. Serve immediately.

Spiced Ginger Snaps

6 servings

¼ cup honey
3 tbsp oil
3 tbsp water or unsweetened
  orange juice
1 cup amaranth flour/ramdana
  ka atta
⅓ cup arrowroot powder/
  paniphal
1 tsp Eno's fruit salt
½ tsp sodium bicarbonate
½ tsp ginger powder/saunth
½ tsp powdered cinnamon/
  dalchini
⅛ tsp powdered cloves/
  lavang

Put the honey, oil and water or orange juice in a large pan over moderate heat and stir till well blended. Remove from heat, and set aside.

Sift the remaining ingredients into a bowl. Stir it into the honey mix.

Drop rounded teaspoonfuls of batter on to a lightly greased baking tray, keeping enough space between them to allow the snaps to spread a little.

Bake in an oven preheated to 150°C for about 15 minutes, till light brown.

Transfer ginger snaps to a wire rack to cool.

Store in an airtight container and use within a few days.

Amaranth Cheesecake

8-10 servings

Base
¾ cup amaranth flour/
  ramdana ka atta
¾ cup wholewheat flour/
  gehun ka atta
1½ tsp baking powder
4 tbsp honey
1 tsp vanilla extract
1 cup milk or water
½ cup chopped walnuts
½ cup chopped almonds

Cheese and pineapple topping
1 fresh pineapple
1 cup grated cottage cheese/
  paneer
1 tbsp honey
1 tsp vanilla extract
Milk as required

Note

If using tinned pineapple, drain it before crushing, and omit the honey.

Base
Sift both the flours with the baking powder into a bowl.

Mix the honey and the vanilla in another bowl. Fold in 2 tbsp of flour and 4 tbsp of milk or water alternately into the bowl containing the honey till all the flour and milk or water are used. Stir in the nuts.

Pour the mix into a lightly greased baking tray dusted with flour.

Bake in an oven preheated to 215°C-220°C for 15-18 minutes, till light brown. Test if done by inserting a thin skewer into the centre of the cake: it should come out clean. Bake for a few minutes longer if necessary.

Turn the cake out on to a wire rack to cool.

Topping
Peel and core the pineapple. Chop the flesh and crush it. Set aside.

Blend the cheese, honey and vanilla in a mixer till it has a thick pouring consistency. Add some milk if needed.

To assemble the cheesecake
Cut the cake into wedges and split each wedge horizontally into half.

Spoon the pineapple on the base of the cake wedges. Pour the cheese topping over it and cover with the top half of the cake wedge.

Amaranth Crêpes with Lemon Sauce

4 servings

Lemon sauce
¼ cup honey
¼ cup lemon or lime juice
1 tbsp amaranth flour
1 tsp finely grated lemon or
   lime peel

Crêpes
3 eggs
1 tsp honey
1 tsp vanilla extract
2 tbsp melted butter or oil
¾ cup milk or water (milk
   tastes better)
⅓ cup amaranth flour/
   ramdana ka atta
A pinch of salt (optional)
Butter for frying
4 table bananas, mashed

Lemon sauce
Combine all the ingredients, except the peel, in a pan over moderate heat. Add 1 cup of water. Simmer, stirring continuously, till it becomes translucent and slightly thick.

Remove from heat and stir in the peel. Keep warm.

Crêpes
Whisk the eggs in a bowl and add the honey, vanilla, butter or oil and milk or water. Mix till well blended.

Sift the flour and salt into another bowl and fold it into the egg mix. Stir to make a smooth batter.

Place a non-stick frying pan over moderate heat till warm. Put ½ tbsp of butter in the pan and swirl it to spread the butter over the base.

Add ½ cup of batter. Swirl the pan to spread the batter and cook the crêpe till light brown at the base. Flip over and cook the other side. Remove the crêpe from the pan.

Spread a layer of mashed bananas along the side of the crêpe and roll to form a cigar.

Make the remaining crêpes in the same way and arrange them side by side on a platter. Spoon the sauce over them and serve at room temperature.

Variation: Mix the mashed bananas with a little cream or whipped paneer. Add some sugar if desired.

Lapsi Kheer (Broken Wheat Dessert)

6-8 servings

¾ cup ghee
1 cup broken wheat/dalia/
  lapsi
¾ cup sugar
- ½ tsp powdered green
  cardamom/chhoti elaichi

Decoration
15 seedless raisins/kishmish
10 almonds, blanched, peeled
  and slivered
10 pistachios/pista, slivered

Soak the raisins in ½ cup of water and set aside.

Put 2 tbsp of the measured ghee in a heavy-based pan over moderate heat. Add the broken wheat and sauté over high heat till it turns pinkish brown.

Pour in 2½ cups of hot water, cover the pan partially and cook over moderate heat till most of the water has evaporated. Test and add more water if the wheat is not tender enough.

Once all the water has evaporated, add the sugar, remaining ghee and ½ cup of water. Stir till well blended.

Sprinkle in the cardamom powder. Place the pan on a tava or griddle over very low heat and cook for 8-10 minutes, stirring occasionally.

The lapsi is ready when the ghee starts oozing out at the sides of the pan.

Serve the lapsi hot, sprinkled with drained raisins, almonds and pistachios.

Meethe Appe (Coconut Semolina Dumplings)

8-10 servings

1 cup grated fresh coconut
1 cup beaten rice/poha
2 cups semolina/rava/sooji
A pinch of salt
½ cup grated jaggery/gud
5-6 green cardamoms/chhoti
  elaichi, powdered
A pinch of sodium
  bicarbonate
1 cup ghee

Note

An appe pan is a round frying
pan with depressions similar to
egg-cups.

Grind the coconut and beaten rice to make a slightly coarse batter. Add the semolina and grind to make a fine batter. Mix in the salt, jaggery and cardamoms and grind for a little longer.

Mix the sodium bicarbonate into the mixture and set aside for 10 minutes.

Place an appe pan over moderate heat and brush each depression with ghee. Fill each depression with some batter. Fry lightly over low to moderate heat, turning the appe over 2-3 times with the help of a knife and fork. Remove when both sides of the appe are golden brown. Drain and place on kitchen paper to absorb excess ghee.

Make the remaining appe in the same way.

Mal Puri (Sweet Semolina and Wheat Flour Pancakes)

10-12 puri

1 litre full-cream milk
4 tbsp super-refined wheat
 flour/maida
3 tbsp semolina/rava/sooji
1 kg sugar
Ghee for frying

Decoration
2 tbsp chopped pistachios/
 pista or any other nuts

Place the milk in a heavy-based pan over high heat and bring to a boil. Lower the heat and simmer till it is reduced to half. Remove from heat and set aside to cool.

Sift the flour into a bowl. Mix in the semolina. Slowly pour in the milk, stirring continuously to make a smooth batter without lumps. Set aside for 10-15 minutes.

Cook the sugar with 5 cups of water to make a slightly thick syrup, the consistency of honey. Remove from heat and set aside.

Smear a small frying pan with ghee and place it over low heat. Pour 1 tbsp of batter into the pan and spread with the back of a spoon to make a 3" round puri. Cook till the base is light brown. Flip over and cook the other side till light brown.

Dip the puri into the sugar syrup to coat completely. Remove and arrange on a platter. Make all the mal puri in the same way.

Sprinkle nuts on top and serve hot.

Jaggery and Wheat Fudge

6-8 servings

1 cup jaggery/gud
1 cup wholewheat flour/gehun ka atta
½ cup + 2 tbsp ghee
10 seedless raisins/kishmish
1 tsp powdered green cardamom/chhoti elaichi

Mix the jaggery with 2 cups of water in a pan and cook over moderate heat till it melts completely and thickens into a syrup. Remove from heat and set aside.

Sift the flour into a bowl.

Put ½ cup of ghee in a heavy-based pan over low heat. Add the flour and roast, tossing all the while for about 15 minutes, till you get the aroma of roasted wheat.

Pour in the jaggery syrup and cook, stirring continuously, till it has a semi-solid consistency. Stir in 2 tbsp of melted ghee, the raisins and cardamom and remove from heat.

Serve at room temperature.

Mandigae (Flaky Biscuits in Sugar Syrup)

10-12 servings

2 cups wholewheat flour/
gehun ka atta

2 tbsp ghee + extra for deep-
frying

1 tsp rice, soaked in water

1 fresh coconut, grated

2 tbsp poppy seeds/
khus-khus

3 green cardamoms/chhoti
elaichi

1¼ cups grated jaggery/gud

Sift the flour into a bowl and rub in 2 tbsp of ghee. Gradually add about ¼ cup of water and knead to prepare a stiff dough as for puri. Roll into thin puri, deep-fry them in oil and set aside (page 126).

Drain the rice and grind it with the coconut, poppy seeds and cardamoms to make a fine paste.

Place the jaggery in a pan over moderate heat with 3 cups of water. Cook over low to moderate heat for 4-5 minutes stirring continuously till the jaggery melts and dissolves.

Add the coconut-rice paste. Cook for 4-5 minutes and remove from heat.

Dip each puri into the syrup to coat completely. Drain and arrange on a serving platter.

Shankarpali (Sweet Pastry Diamonds)

4 servings

2½ cups wholewheat flour/
  gehun ka atta + extra for
  rolling
½ cup sugar
1 cup milk
A pinch of salt
¼ cup ghee + extra for deep-
  frying

Sift the flour into a bowl. Add the remaining ingredients, except the ghee for deep-frying. Mix well and knead to prepare a stiff dough. Set aside for 2 hours.

Divide the dough into portions the size of a tennis ball. Roll into roti the size of a dinner plate on a lightly floured surface.

Place one roti on a cutting board and cut into 1" strips from left to right. Turn the board by 45 degrees and repeat the process so that you get 1" diamonds.

Put the ghee for deep-frying in a kadhai or wok over moderate heat. When hot, fry the shankarpali in batches till they float to the surface and turn golden. Drain and place on kitchen paper to absorb excess ghee.

Cool and store in an airtight container.

Puran Poli (Pastry with a Sweet Bengal Gram Filling)

20 servings

1 cup super-refined wheat flour/maida + extra for rolling
A pinch of turmeric powder/haldi
A pinch of salt
2 tsp ghee
6 tbsp oil + extra for frying

Filling
1¼ cups husked Bengal gram/chana dal
1½ cups grated jaggery/gud
¼ tsp powdered green cardamom/chhoti elaichi

Sift the flour into a bowl. Add the turmeric powder, salt and ghee and mix well. Gradually add about ¼ cup of water and knead to prepare a smooth, soft dough. Cover with a damp cloth or cling film and set aside for 40-50 minutes.

Knead again. Add 6 tbsp of oil to the dough and knead till the oil is completely absorbed. Cover the dough and set aside for 4 hours.

Wash the dal and pressure-cook it with 2 cups of water for 15 minutes after the cooker reaches full pressure. Allow the cooker to cool and put the dal in a colander to drain thoroughly.

Grind the dal with the jaggery and cardamom to make a fine, dry crumbly paste. The filling should not be watery.

Divide the filling into marble-sized balls. Divide the dough into walnut-sized balls and flatten them into discs in the palms of your hands.

Place a ball of filling in the centre of each disc. Fold the dough over the filling to cover it completely, and press the top to seal it, using a little water if required. Shape into balls.

Carefully roll out the balls, on a lightly floured surface into thick, 5" round polya, ensuring that the filling does not leak out.

Place a tava or griddle over moderate heat. When hot, place a poli on it. When brown spots appear on the base, smear a little oil on the surface and turn it over to roast the other side. Smear some more oil on the surface of the cooked side.

Cool and serve at room temperature.

Gehun Laddu (Wheat Fudge)

Makes 15-20 Laddu

1 cup wholewheat flour/gehun
ka atta
1 cup + 1 cup ghee
1 cup fine sugar
½ cup seedless raisins/
kishmish
5-6 green cardamom/chhoti
elaichi, powdered

Sift the flour into a heavy-based pan. Rub in 1 cup of ghee.

Place the pan over low heat and cook till the flour turns light brown and you get the aroma of roasted wheat.

Remove from heat and set aside to cool for about 5 minutes.

While still warm, mix in the sugar, raisins and cardamoms.

Roll into balls to make Laddus. Add 1 tbsp of ghee at a time, while rolling them, as the mixture tends to get dry.

Cool and store in airtight containers.

Dudh Pitti (Wheat Porridge)

12 servings

1 cup wholewheat flour/gehun ka atta + extra for dusting
¼ cup + 1 litre milk
1 tsp ghee
½ cup sugar
1 tsp powdered green cardamom/chhoti elaichi
2 tsp rose water/gulabjal

Sift 1 cup of flour into a bowl. Add ¼ cup of milk and mix well. Gradually add up to ¼ cup of water and knead to prepare a stiff dough.

Dust your fingertips with flour and pinch off small balls of dough the size of rice grains. Spread the balls on a clean surface to dry for about 30 minutes.

Heat the ghee in a large frying pan over low heat and toss the balls in the ghee till pink. Set aside.

Place a heavy-based pan with 1 litre of milk over high heat and add the roasted balls. Bring to a boil and continue boiling till the milk is reduced by a third.

Stir in the sugar and cardamom. Remove from heat and allow to cool.

Sprinkle in rose water and mix well.

Serve chilled.

Jhangora Phirni (Barnyard Millet Custard)

10-12 servings

2 cups barnyard millet grains/
   jhangora/samak
2 litres milk
2 cups sugar
A pinch of saffron strands/
   kesar

Decoration
¼ cup cashew nuts, chopped
¼ cup seedless raisins/
   kishmish, chopped

Clean the millet grains, wash, drain and set aside.

Place the milk in a heavy-based pan over high heat and bring to a boil.

Add the millet to the milk. Cook till the millet is tender, stirring frequently to avoid lumps.

Add the sugar and cook till it dissolves.

Mix the saffron in a teaspoon of warm milk taken from the pan and pour it into the phirni.

Serve hot or chilled, sprinkled with the chopped nuts and raisins.

Gud Papdi (Jaggery Brittle)

Makes about 200 gms of brittle

½ tsp poppy seeds/khus-khus
½ cup wholewheat flour/
   gehun ka atta
4 tbsp ghee
1/3 cup grated jaggery/gud
¼ tsp powdered green
   cardamom/chhoti elaichi

Sprinkle the poppy seeds on a lightly greased 4" round thali (a flat metal plate with a low rim) and set aside.

Sift the flour into a heavy-based pan. Add the ghee and mix till well blended. Place the pan over low heat and cook, stirring continuously, till it turns golden brown.

Add the jaggery and cardamom and continue to stir, till the jaggery melts and the ingredients are well blended.

Pour the contents of the pan into the thali, and spread it evenly with the back of a spoon.

Cut the gud papdi into diamond-shaped pieces and set aside till cool.

Separate the pieces and store in an airtight container.

Shrikand (Rich Yogurt Dessert)

6-8 servings

3 litres milk
1 tsp yogurt/dahi
Caster sugar equal in volume
   to the hung yogurt
A pinch of saffron strands
A pinch of freshly ground
   nutmeg/jaiphal
¼ tsp powdered green
   cardamom

Decoration
1½ tsp cudpah nuts/charoli/
   chironji
1½ tsp pistachios/pista

Bring the milk to a boil, remove from heat and cool till lukewarm.

Transfer the milk to a bowl and mix in the yogurt. Stir lightly, cover the bowl with a lid and leave it overnight to set into thick yogurt.

The next morning, pour the yogurt into a strainer lined with thin muslin. Hang the yogurt in the muslin cloth for 1-2 hours to drain. Place a bowl under the bag to collect the drippings.

Measure the volume of hung yogurt in the muslin and transfer it to a bowl. Add an equal volume of caster sugar and mix well.

Press the mixture through a thin cloth or strainer.

Blend in the saffron, nutmeg and cardamom.

Transfer to a serving bowl and sprinkle the nuts on top.

Serve chilled.

Variations:
• Shrikand can be made without saffron.
• Fresh fruit can be mixed into the shrikand before serving.

Tilgul (Sesame Seed, Peanut Brittle)

Makes about 1 kg of brittle

5 cups white sesame seeds/til
¼ cup shredded dried coconut/kopra
¼ cup shelled, peeled peanuts, coarsely crushed
2½ cups grated jaggery/gud (the sticky variety)
1 tsp ghee + extra for rolling
8 green cardamoms/chhoti elaichi, powdered

Roast the sesame seeds in a large, heavy-based frying pan over low heat, tossing continuously, till light golden. Remove from heat and set aside.

Roast the coconut and peanuts separately in the same pan over moderate heat, tossing continuously, till light brown. Remove from heat and set aside.

Heat the jaggery in a heavy-based, non-stick pan, over moderate heat, stirring occasionally, till the jaggery melts.

Add 1 tsp of ghee and stir till well blended.

When the jaggery starts to bubble and turns light red, stir in the sesame seeds, coconut, peanuts and cardamom and remove from heat. The mixture should be slightly sticky and thick.

Rub some ghee on your palms. While the mixture is still hot, but cool enough to handle, roll into 1" balls. If the mixture gets cold, heat it lightly to make the rolling easier.

Set aside till cool. They will turn hard and crisp.

Store in an airtight container.

Til Poli (Sweet Sesame Bread)

Makes 10-12 polya

1½ cups super-refined wheat flour/maida
1½ tbsp oil + extra for shallow-frying

Filling
2 cups white sesame seeds/til
2 cups grated jaggery/gud
1½ tsp powdered green cardamom/chhoti elaichi
¼ tsp freshly grated nutmeg/ jaiphal

Sift the flour and salt into a bowl. Add 1½ tbsp of oil and knead to prepare a soft dough. Cover with a damp cloth or cling film and set aside for an hour.

Roast the sesame seeds in a large, dry, heavy-based frying pan over low heat, tossing continuously, till light golden brown. Remove from heat and set aside.

When cool, grind them coarsely. Add the jaggery and grind once more to make the mixture even and smooth.

Mix the cardamom and nutmeg together in a bowl and stir it into the sesame-jaggery mix.

Pinch off lemon-sized balls of dough.

Place a ball in your left palm and make an indentation in the centre. Put 1 tsp of the sesame-jaggery mix into the hollow.

Fold the dough over the filling to cover it completely, and press the top to seal it, using a little water if required.

Smear a wooden board with oil, place a ball on it and roll out into as thin a round as possible.

Make the remaining polya in the same way.

Smear a little oil on a tava or griddle and cook each poli on both sides till deep golden and crisp.

Serve warm or at room temperature.

Til Khoya Laddu (Sesame Seed Fudge)

Makes 30-40 Laddu

1½ cups sesame seeds/til
2 cups khoya/mawa
 (unsweetened milk solids)
5 tbsp powdered sugar

Decoration
2 strands saffron/kesar
2 tbsp blanched, peeled and
 chopped almonds
10 pistachios/pista,
 chopped

Roast the sesame seeds in a large, dry, heavy-based frying pan over low heat, tossing continuously, till light golden brown. Remove from heat and set aside till cool. Grind them coarsely.

Roast the khoya in a pan over low heat till it is a very light golden. Let it cool for a few minutes and add the sesame seeds.

Add the sugar when the mixture is lukewarm. (If the mixture is too hot the sugar will melt.) Mix well and shape into small balls. Set aside till cool.

Arrange the Laddu on a plate, sprinkle saffron and nuts over them and serve or store in an airtight container.

Nariyal Barfi (Coconut Fudge)

Makes about 40 barfi

1 cup grated fresh coconut,
 ground to a paste
2½ cups sugar
6 cups full-cream milk
2 tsp vanilla extract
A few drops permitted food
 colouring of choice
 (optional)

Decoration
2 tbsp blanched, peeled and
 chopped almonds
2 tbsp chopped pistachios/
 pista

Mix the coconut, sugar and milk in a heavy-based pan. Cook over high heat till it thickens to a dropping consistency.

Mix in the vanilla and food colouring (if used). Pour into a greased thali (a flat metal plate with a low rim) and cut into cubes when cool.

Sprinkle the nuts over them.

Store in an airtight container.

Coconut Ice Cream

8-10 servings

1 tbsp cornflour
2 tbsp cold milk
1½ litres full-cream milk
1 cup sugar
50 gms soft khoya/mawa
   (unsweetened milk solids),
   crumbled
½ tsp vanilla extract
1 cup powdered dried
   coconut/kopra
1 cup fresh cream, whisked
1 tsp instant coffee powder

Mix the cornflour and cold milk together in a bowl and set aside.

Boil the full-cream milk in a large, heavy-based pan over high heat. Lower the heat and simmer for about 20 minutes, stirring occasionally.

Add the cornflour paste and sugar, stirring continuously.

Mix in the khoya. Simmer, stirring frequently, till the mixture is thick enough to coat the back of the spoon.

Add the vanilla. Remove from heat and cool to room temperature, stirring occasionally.

Pour the mixture into an ice cream tray and cover with aluminium foil.

Place it in the freezer till it is firm, but not hard.

Transfer the ice cream to a large bowl and beat it with a wooden spoon or eggbeater till it is soft and fluffy, but do not allow it to melt.

Return to the ice cream tray and replace in the freezer to reset.

Repeat the process of beating the ice cream once more.

Mix in the coconut powder and cream and beat well. Transfer to the ice cream tray, cover and set till firm.

Serve scoops of ice cream, topped with a sprinkling of instant coffee powder.

Glossary

Glossary

English	Hindi	English	Hindi
Ajwain	*see notes*	Cardamom	
Almond	Badam	-Black	Badi elaichi
Amaranth		-Green	Hari/chhoti elaichi
-Fresh leaves	Cholai bhaaji	Carrot	Gaajar
-Grains	Ramdana	Cashew nut	Kaju
Aniseed	Saunf	Cauliflower	Phool gobhi
Apple	Seb	Chickpeas	Kabuli/safaid chana
Arrowroot	Paniphal	Chilli	Mirchi
Asafoetida	Hing	-dried red	Sookhi mirch
Aubergine/brinjal	Baingan	-Green	Hari mirch
Banana	Kela	Cinnamon	Dalchini
Bay leaf	Tej patta	Clove	Laung
Bell pepper/capsicum	Shimla mirch	Coconut	
Bengal gram		-Copra (dry)	Kopra
-Flour	Besan	-Fresh	Nariyal
-Gram flour strings	Shev	-Milk	Nariyal ka doodh
-Husked	Chana dal	Coriander	Dhania
-Roasted	Bhuna chana	-Fresh	Hara dhania
-Whole	Kala chana	-whole seeds	Sabut dhania
Black beans/ gram		Corn	Makkai
-Husked	Urad dal	–Cob	Bhutta
-Whole	Sabut urad	–Meal	Makki ka atta
Black cumin seeds	Kala jeera / shahi jeera	Cottage cheese	Paneer
		Cream	Malai
Black pepper	Kali miri	Cucumber	Kheera/kakdi
Black salt	Kala namak	Cudpah nut (see notes)	Chironji/charoli
Bottle gourd	Ghia/lauki		
Bread	Double roti	Cumin seeds	Jeera
Brown beans/gram	Matki/moth	-Black cumin	Kala/shah jeera
Brinjal/aubergine	Baingan	Curry leaf	Kari patta
Buckwheat	Kutu	Date	Khajur
Butter	Makkhan	Dill	Sua bhaaji
-Clarified	Ghee	Drumsticks	Surjan ki phalli
Buttermilk	Chhaas	Egg	Anda
Cabbage	Band gobhi	Egyptian/ red lentils	
Capsicum/bell pepper	Shimla mirch	-Husked	Masoor dal

English	Hindi	English	Hindi
Fennel		Mustard	
-Leaves	Sua bhaji	-Greens	Sarson ka saag
Fenugreek		-Seeds	Sarson/rai
-Dry leaves	Kasuri methi	Nutmeg	Jaiphal
-Fresh leaves	Methi bhaji	Oats	Jai
-Whole seeds	Methi dana	Oil	Tael
Fig	Anjeer	Okra/ladies fingers	Bhindi
Finger/ hill millet	Ragi/nachni/	Onion	Pyaaz
	madua/mohuva	Orange	Santra
Garlic	Lassun	Peppercorn	Kali miri
Ginger		Pigeon peas/yellow	Arhar/tuvar
-Dry	Saunth	lentils	
-Fresh	Adrak	Pineapple	Annanas
Green beans/ gram		Pistachios	Pista
-Husked	Mung dal	Pomegranate	
-Split	Chilke mung dal	-Dry seeds	Anardana
-Whole	Sabut mung	Poppy seeds	Khus-khus
Green peas	Mattar	Potato	Alu
Groundnut	Mungphali	Pumpkin	
Honey	Madh/shahad	-Red/yellow	Kaddu
Horse gram	Kulthi ka dal	Radish	
Horse radish	Safaid mooli	-White	Safaid mooli
Indian sour plum	Kokum	Raisin	
Jaggery	Gud	-Seedless	Kishmish
Kidney beans	Rajma	Rice	Chaval
Ladies fingers/okra	Bhindi	-Flour	Chaval ka atta
Lentil	Dal	-Parched/Beaten	Poha
Lime	Limbu/nimbu	-Puffed	Murmura
Mango	Aam	Rose water	Gulabjal
-Powder	Amchur	Saffron	Kesar/zafran
Marrow	Ghia/lauki	Salt	Namak
Milk	Doodh	Semolina	Sooji/rava
Millet		Sesame seeds	Til
-Barnyard	Jhangora	Sodium bicarbonate	Meetha soda
-Finger/hill	Madua/mohuva/	Soybeans	Bhatt
	ragi	Spinach	Palak
-Pearl	Bajra	Spring onion	Hara pyaaz
Milo/sorghum	Jowar	Sugar	Cheeni/shakkar
Mint	Pudina		
Mushroom	Dhingri/khumi		

English	Hindi
Tamarind	Imli
Tomato	Tamatar
Turmeric	Haldi
Vermicelli	Sevian
Vinegar	Sirka
Walnut	Akhrot
Wheat	Gehun
-Broken/cracked/ burgul/lapsi	Dalia/lapsi
-Plain/refined flour	Maida
-Wholewheat flour	Atta
Yeast Khameer	Khameer
Yogurt	Dahi

Notes

Ajwain: It is an umbelliferous plant which grows in India and the Far East. It is sometimes referred to as carom seeds, and belongs to the same family as the Ethiopian bishop's weed and English lovage.

Cudpah nut: Small nuts generally used to garnish sweets; its botanical name is *Buchanania latifolia*.

Khoya: Unsweetened, dried, milk solids made by cooking milk, stirring constantly till it forms a heavy, thick granular lump.

Kokum: The botanical name for kokum is *Garcina indica*. It is also called the Indian sour plum and is used as a souring agent for curries in a number of Indian cuisines. Tamarind may be used as a substitute.

Basil, celery, thyme: These ingredients have no Indian names but are readily available in speciality shops.

Index